D0038863

BORN TO TALK

Thelma E. Weeks

Center for Cross-Cultural Research
Palo Alto, California

Newbury House Publishers, Inc. / Rowley / Massachusetts / 01969

Library of Congress Cataloging in Publication Data

Weeks, Thelma E.
    Born to talk.

    Includes bibliographies and index.
    1. Children--Language.   2. Nonverbal
communication.   I. Title.
P118.W37   401'.9   78-23207
ISBN 0-88377-153-5

NEWBURY HOUSE PUBLISHERS, INC.

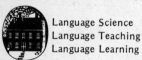
Language Science
Language Teaching
Language Learning

ROWLEY, MASSACHUSETTS 01969

Cover design by KATHE HARVEY

Copyright © 1979 by Newbury House Publishers, Inc. All rights reserved. No
part of this book may be reproduced or transmitted in any form or by any
means, electronic or mechanical, including photocopying, recording, or by
any information storage and retrieval system, without permission in writing
from the Publisher.

First printing: May 1979

Printed in the U.S.A.   5   4   3   2   1

TO
Fred, John, Leslie,
Greg, Jennie, *and* Brandon
Talkers All!
And Kara
An Almost Talker

Contents

SYMBOLS USED

æ	h*a*t
ʌ	c*u*t
i	m*e*
ɛ	l*e*t
e	m*ay*
ə	an unstressed vowel, as in app*e*tite
ɪ	s*i*t
a	h*o*t
ɔ	l*aw*
ʃ	*sh*
?	glottal stop, as in ?oh ?oh
ŋ	si*ng*
ʰ	a noticeable exhalation of air
2:10	two years, ten months of age

Introduction

The Study of Child Language

From the beginning of recorded history, men and women have been interested, for a variety of reasons, in how children learn language. A principal interest in child language stems from the assumption that its study will shed some light on adult language. Until recently, language produced by children was viewed as an imperfect adult system—a system in which children were making a great many mistakes at first but gradually becoming better and better at producing what they were supposed to produce—adult language. In our present state of enlightenment, we realize that children do not begin by producing adult language and doing a poor job of it—they produce child language and do a good job of it. They listen to a very select variety of adult language—the simplified language that is directed to them—and evolve their own language. It is not adult language, but it works. It does for them what language is supposed to do for the speaker: it expresses feelings, it persuades people to do things, it entertains, it sounds nice to the ear, and once in a while it even informs.

This book is about how children learn to produce language that works—how to communicate what they intend to communicate. To a certain extent, this involves using the same words that adults use and the same sentence structures adults use, but there is much more to the learning task than that. The child must learn to use language that is appropriate for the time and the occasion. A three-year-old must learn that it is appropriate to use baby talk with a six-month-old baby or with pets, but not in addressing a strange adult. Even though we realize that a young child devotes much of his energy during the first few years of life to mastering language, we are amazed that a two-and-a-half-year-old has learned to say to his grandfather, by way of making polite conversation, "It's chilly today, isn't it?"; to his mother who has just put him into bath water that is too hot, "Are we too warm?"; and to a playmate of his own age, "Gimme that truck." Linguists have not yet been able to formulate rules that are complex enough to specify the many ways language needs to be varied for the situations an ordinary speaker finds himself in almost any day, but young children, being born talkers, learn to do it.

The Reader

This book is for anyone who likes children or is interested in how children acquire language and use it. Primarily, it is for a general audience (individuals with little or no linguistic background); however, I have used this material as a text for upper-division and graduate-level university courses I have taught. It is my intention to present the material in such a way that anyone will be able to understand it but to include material of sufficient substance that individuals with a considerable linguistic background will also find it stimulating. For nonspecialists, I have tried to keep technical terminology and jargon to a minimum. Suggested readings are given with each chapter, and a glossary is included at the end of the book.

Sources of Data

There are two major sources of data for this book. First is the extensive body of literature currently becoming available on the aspects of child language discussed here. I have reviewed this literature and reported on it.

The second source of data is my own research, which is of two types. First is my work with a group of seven children whose language development I have been following for most of their lifetimes. The children come from four homes: Fred and Leslie are siblings; John, Greg, and Jennie are siblings; Brandon is an only child, and so is Kara. Fred and Leslie are cousins of John, Greg, and Jennie, but Brandon and Kara, who are cared for during the day by Fred and Leslie's mother (Barb), are not related to them or to each other. Both Leslie and Jennie were adopted, Leslie at two months and Jennie, a Korean child, at five months. At this writing Fred is 13:5 (13 years and 5 months of age), John is 11:6, Leslie 10:0, Greg 7:11, Jennie 5:7, Brandon 1:10, and Kara 1:0.

The parents in all four families are college-educated and child-oriented, so that the children may be thought of as being reared under nearly ideal circumstances. The children do not represent a random sample, nor do I assume they are "average," whatever that may be. They are, however, normal, and perhaps by merest chance, individualistic in their language-acquisition patterns. If we think that because of their similar home environments, they will acquire language similarly, we will be disappointed. While there are many aspects of their acquisition patterns that fall neatly into universal patterns, "my seven children" offer a fascinating study in contrasts.

The data have been gathered at rather irregular intervals by means of audio-tape recordings plus written notes. Some of this material has been reported elsewhere.[1] A persistent attempt has been made to observe the children in a variety of settings with a variety of kinds of special language tasks. For example, the children have been observed at all hours of the day, while eating, bathing, playing; in many places such as their home, my home, parks, airports, and restaurants; and talking to family members and strangers of all ages as well as to pets. I have given the older children a wide variety of language tasks, such as asking them to converse on specific topics, retell stories, make up stories, produce tag questions for a list of sentences I read to them, respond to Lewis Carroll's "Jabberwocky," take the Peabody Picture Vocabulary Test, the Berko-Gleason Morphology Test, etc.

The second type of research I have conducted, and have drawn upon for this book, is with the Yakima Indian children who live on a reservation in central Washington. I began my work there in 1968, and during the past 10 years have tried to learn the native language (Sahaptin), have visited children in their homes, and have worked with other children in a preschool nursery program that was conducted by Yakima adults. Most of the Yakima children, I should mention, are monolingual English speakers. Even children who have Sahaptin-speaking grandparents living in the home speak little Sahaptin, for the older generation has learned to understand English whether they speak it well or not.

The Use of Tape Recorders

For the reader who wonders if a child's language is "natural" while the tape recorder is grinding away, I would like to point out that the seven children whose language I follow regularly became accustomed to having microphones and tape-recording equipment around them long before they knew what they were for. It was never a novelty to them, and if it seemed sometimes to be a nuisance, it also seemed to be worth it to them because what went with it was an attentive adult. They all seemed to enjoy it and habitually asked, "Can we tape?" (Taping has lost its charm by now for John and Fred, but there are still occasional situations in which they are willing to talk.) On the Yakima Reservation, I always spent a good amount of time getting acquainted with children before introducing any equipment. On home visits, I did not do any recording on the first visit, and waited until the children seemed to feel comfortable on the second visit before recording. Likewise, in the nursery school, I spent a couple of days getting acquainted before I brought out my equipment.

Some Yakima adults warned me that the children might be a little bit shy, but I found their shyness lasted for about 30 seconds. After that, they were veritable chatterboxes vying for a chance to talk. The children I have worked with have certainly not been intimidated by recording equipment. Wherever I find children—on the Yakima Indian Reservation, in nursery schools, or at home—I find that they enjoy an adult's undiluted concentration on them for an hour or two at a time.

Thanks are due to several individuals. I want to thank Rupert Ingram of Newbury House for suggesting the title of this book. Special thanks go to Courtney B. Cazden for her careful reading of the manuscript and for making many valuable suggestions regarding both content and organization. To the extent to which I followed her suggestions, the book is much improved; the extent to which the manuscript falls short of the ideal is entirely my doing.

My principal gratitude regarding this volume must go to "my seven children," particularly the older ones, who have tolerated my listening, questioning, talking, tagging after, and testing, with good nature. The insight I have gained into how children actually acquire language has come from working closely with these children, who became aware at early ages that I was particularly interested in their language, and became partners with me in the investigation. Sometimes they even reported their progress to me; for example, Leslie volunteered, "Know-what? I used to say /ɛfənənt/. Now I say *elephant*!"

I also wish to thank the parents for their generosity in allowing me such free access to their children, and for calling to my attention aspects of the children's language development that I might not have noticed otherwise. In addition the parents have read and commented on the chapters of this book.

Claudette Bolter deserves special thanks for her typing, editing, and help with the index for the manuscript.

Finally, I want to thank my husband, Robert L. Weeks, for his patience, editing, suggestions, and constant encouragement, without which I could not have written the book at all.

July 10, 1978
Palo Alto, California

NOTES

1. Weeks, Thelma E. "Speech Registers in Young Children," *Child Development*, 1971, 42:1119-1131; *The Slow Speech Development of a Bright Child*, Lexington, Mass.: Lexington Books, D.C. Heath, 1974; "The Use of Nonverbal Communication by a Slow Speech Developer," in *Child Language—1975*, edited by Walburga von Raffler-Engel, International Linguistic Association, 1976, special issue of *Word*, 1971, 27:460-472; "Some Paralinguistic and Registral Patterns in the Speech of Yakima Indian Children," paper presented at the Western Regional Meeting of the American Dialect Society, San Jose State University, May 3, 1975.

BORN TO TALK

1

Functions of Language

Why do children learn to talk? That question may be almost as redundant as asking why is a child a child, for we know that all normal children growing up in a normal environment learn to talk. We are born to talk. In this age of computers, we may think of ourselves as having been programmed to talk. Children do not set out to learn words or to produce sentences; they set out to accomplish something, and language is the tool. In this respect, function seems to precede language. When children have something they want to do, they find a way to do it, and the principal thing they want to do with language is communicate. Noncommunicative uses of language are vital, but communication is generally considered to be the primary purpose of language.[1]

> Leslie, aged 3 years, 2 months (3:2), had a pile of colored blocks of various sizes and shapes with which she was playing house.
> Leslie: I can't find one. That cracked, too.
> Weeks: Yes, it looks like it is cracked, or almost cracked.
> Leslie: This ... I need this side not crack. Hey, I need ... oh ... one ... these not beds.

Weeks: They're not beds? (I helped her look for other
 blocks.)
Leslie: Uh uh. (No.)
Weeks: What is it?
Leslie: I make sumping.
Weeks: What is it?
Leslie: /inink idink baek/ (You lean back.)
Weeks: You want me to sit back?
Leslie: Yeah.
Weeks: Why?
Leslie: Cuz.
Weeks: I was trying to get close to see what you were doing.
Leslie: /i ʌ/ sit back watch me. (You just sit back and
 watch me.)

Children do things with their language. In this exchange, Leslie got help
in finding the right kind of blocks: "I can't find one," means "Find one
for me," and "I need this side not crack," means "Find one for me that's
not cracked." In the next exchange, in which I was trying to find out if
the blocks were not beds, what they were, she tried to discourage my
attention with "I make sumping." This was her polite brushoff, meaning
leave me alone, but I didn't take the hint, so she had to be more direct.
But she continued to use language to get me out of her way. She could
have pushed me back, but aside from being the more civilized way,
language is a very effective way of getting others to do what you want
them to do.

 Child-Language Functions   Anyone who has been around children
has undoubtedly noted that children make a variety of uses of language.
They use it to get attention, to persuade someone to do something for
them, to talk to their pet, to entertain themselves, etc. However, there is
no general agreement among child-language researchers as to just what
should be named as functions of child language. Sometimes functions
that appear to be the same are given different labels, and researchers do
not agree that children use language for the same purposes. There is
rather general agreement, however, that children may direct their speech
either to others or to themselves; that is, they may use communicative or
noncommunicative language. But given any one specific utterance of a
particular child, there may not be agreement on how it should be
categorized. For example, Brandon (1:11), who had been looking at a
picture book by himself, saw a picture of a cow, and said "cow." He kept
turning pages which had pictures of other things on them. A few minutes

later, he was apparently looking for the picture of the cow again and could not find it, so he yelled, "Hey, cow!" Now, how should this utterance be classified? I shall leave that to you, the reader, to solve, and hope that this chapter stimulates you to look at child language in a new way—to think about what children are trying to accomplish when they talk—to ask different questions from those you have been accustomed to asking about children's language.

The ten communicative functions and seven noncommunicative functions discussed in this chapter represent a synthesis of those mentioned in the literature on child language. The first seven functions of language (see Table 1) are from Halliday,[2] who contends that the

Table 1 Communicative Functions of Language

Name of function	How child uses it	Examples from child speech
1. Instrumental	Makes requests to fulfill needs. Protests	I need a cookie! No!
2. Regulatory (conative, self-maintaining)*	To control activities of others	Sit back and watch me
3. Interactional (phatic, encounter regulation, contact)	Greeting, issues summons to talk, keeps channels of communication open	Hewo, widdo Miss Pretty, Byebye Know what?
4. Personal (relational, emotive, expressive, interpersonal)	Expresses feelings, and individuality	You're funny Yukky!
5. Heuristic	Explores reality, uses language for learning	Why are the doors locked?
6. Imaginative	Plays games, makes up stories in interaction with others	Peekaboo! Let's play house
7. Informational (representational, referential, denotative)	Offers information that the listener does not have, and makes comments	I went to the store today
8. Poetic (aesthetics)	Focuses on the message for its own sake	He put him in a little boat, little boaty boat
9. Interpretive (reminiscent, projective)	Recalls experiences, plans experiences, solves problems, interprets experiences	I took some trucks to the park last time. What can I take this time?
10. Performative	Promises, bets	I'll be good!

*Terms enclosed in parentheses are those used by other writers for the same or a similar function.

young child tends to use language in just one function at a time only at the earliest stages of language development, whereas "with the adult almost every instance of language involves all functions at once, in subtle and complex interactions." Because of this, most examples in this chapter are from the earliest stages. Even then, we will see that interpretation is not always simple and often involves two or more functions.

Most of the communicative functions are discussed further in Chapter 2. Imaginative and poetic functions (communicative) and language play (noncommunicative) are discussed further in Chapter 3. How various of these functions are accomplished by nonverbal rather than verbal means is discussed further in Chapter 4.

Communicative Functions of Language

Communicative, or socialized speech, is language that is directed to others rather than to one's self—language that is adapted to the hearer. Piaget[3] found that somewhat more than half of the language produced by the children he observed was socialized, but most researchers in the United States in this decade find a much higher proportion of communicative to noncommunicative speech.[4]

Instrumental Function   This is the function children are using when they say "I want it!" "I need it!" or "I don't want it!" It is the function that is used to fulfill desires and needs, and for making protests. Any caretaker of a baby will recognize that this is, as Halliday mentions, one of the first to evolve. Ways of expressing desires and needs develop much earlier than words of any formal language structure; in this case, at least, function precedes structure. Before a child can say "I don't want it!" or even "No!" the child can push away a proffered spoonful of food or unwanted toy. One of the needs a child can make known to the caretaker at a very early age is for food. Mothers soon learn to tell the difference between a cry that indicates the baby is hungry, angry, or tired, etc. Desires (as opposed to needs) are also made known before the child has language to use. When Kara was 13 months old, she and Brandon sometimes played ball. She let him know that she wanted him to throw her the ball first by stretching out her arms, and if the ball was not forthcoming immediately, she cried. At this writing, she has not yet learned to say "Throw me the ball!" but her actions plus her crying made her desires easily understood.

Once a child is producing language, child-language researchers have noted that a large proportion of early utterances are imperatives: "Milk!"

"No shoes!" "Gimme cookie!" The instrumental function, by its very nature, makes extensive use of the imperative form. Such requests are usually very clear; when Kara said "Cheese!" (0:10 to 1:0), no one doubted what she wanted. Sometimes, however, requests require some interpretation. At 1:4, Kara saw her mother drinking some coffee, and repeated, "faffee, faffee, faffee!" Her mother was puzzled that she wanted some coffee, but then discovered she simply wanted something to drink. She was thirsty, and had observed that her mother was drinking something.

This is perhaps the easiest of all functions to classify accurately.

Regulatory Function   This function is similar to the instrumental except that the instrumental is used by the child to satisfy his own material needs and the regulatory is used to exert control over the behavior of others in various ways. In trying to analyze the speech of older children who are taking care of more of their own needs and making fewer such need-demands on others, it might be more practical to combine these two functions. The regulatory function, as well as the instrumental, makes extensive use of imperative sentences: "Watch me!" "Give me a turn!" "Put on my sweater!" etc. At 1:0 Brandon said, as he handed me a book, /i dɪ/ (Read it!), and at 1:8, to his mother, "Mom, sit down!", clear efforts to regulate the behavior of others.

The examples at the beginning of this chapter of Leslie's telling me to lean back and then to sit back were typical of the regulatory function, making use of imperatives. (It is not unusual at this stage of development for imperatives to include the second person pronoun in initial position in the imperative—Leslie's multipurpose function word /i/ seemed to be a substitute for "you." Although this form is not routine for adults, the child does hear examples of it, such as "You come here right now!" where the initial pronoun is used for emphasis.) However, the regulatory function includes many directives (see Chapter 2) that are couched in a more polite form, such as her first and second utterances, which I interpreted to be requests for help. Her "I make sumping" may also have been a hint that I did not interpret correctly. At early ages, it is often necessary to consider the entire situation and the child's nonverbal behavior before determining what a child's intentions may be in speaking. When Jennie was 2:3, for example, she saw her mother was getting ready to go out, and she said, "Ma. Go?" She reached up to take her mother's hand and made it clear she wanted to go to the store with her mother, as she often did. On the same day, she saw her father getting ready to go and said, "Da. Go?" She made no move to go with him, but waved good-bye as soon as he got to the door. Her first "Go?" might be interpreted as "Take me!" or more politely, "May I go?" while the question directed to her father was simply a request for information about what he was doing, and would probably be classified as interactional.

As we will see repeatedly, a child expresses himself first in nonverbal ways, then in verbal ways later. For example, the snap on Brandon's pant leg came undone when he was 0:10. He looked expectantly at Barb, and when she did not snap it for him, he grabbed at the pant leg as he continued to look at her. She snapped it for him and he went away satisfied. If he had been a little older, he might have asked, "Fix this" or "Would you please snap my pants?" but at 0:10, he made his request known without language. The communicative intention is the same, with or without the structure of language.

Interactional Function   This is the third function noted by Halliday, and he comments,[5] "This refers to the use of language in the interaction between the self and others. Even the closest of the child's personal relationships, that with his mother, is partly and in time largely mediated through language; his interaction with other people, adults and children, is very obviously maintained linguistically. (Those who come nearest to achieving a personal relationship that is not linguistically mediated, apparently are twins.)" In the neighborhood and in peer groups, language is used to define and consolidate the group, to exclude and to include, to make clear just who belongs to the "in-group." Greetings and summons to speak (discussed in Chapter 2) as well as farewells and other routines used in conversation are also included in this function.

A routine that Leslie used frequently for starting conversations was "Know what?" As soon as she had my attention, she would go on to talk about whatever she had on her mind. Gregory was more direct. "Let's talk about . . ." was a favorite way for him to start a conversation. At 3:8, for example, when his parents were preparing to move to San Diego, he repeatedly asked, "Let's talk about San Diego." At prelanguage stages, children often try to establish an interchange nonverbally. From 1:5 to 2:1 Brandon, for example, regularly came to me, took my hand, and led me to some toys. If I continued to stand, he tugged on my arm, indicating he wanted me to sit down and play with him. This qualifies as regulatory, in that he was trying to get me to do something, but ultimately, what he wanted was to interact with me. So again, we can see how the semantics of the situation is present before there is language; it is expressed differently before and after language is available to the child.

By the time Brandon was 1:11, he was producing a great deal of language and was not relying so much on nonverbal means of getting attention. For example, I had been staying with him and Kara, and Fred and his mother came in the door. Brandon was excited to see them, and immediately shouted "My dit! My dit!" (I did! I did!). If he had done something and was trying to report it to them, it would have been counted as the use of the informational function, but it was not at all clear what he had done. His objective seemed to be to get the attention of Fred and Barb away from Kara, who was crying.

A more dubious case is that of Kara, who at 1:0, habitually said /dæ/ (Daddy) whenever the phone rang. At home, when the phone rang, her mother would say, "I wonder if that's Daddy." So during the day, at Fred and Leslie's house, she seemed to be repeating what her mother said at home. Was she talking to herself or to another person in the room? She did not seem to expect a response, nor did her mother when she asked the question. She may have considered it the friendly thing to say when the phone rang, in which case we might say it was an attempt on Kara's part to interact with Barb. We will never know for sure.

Jakobson[6] includes in this function attempts to prolong a conversation, or talking without saying anything, such as the following Dorothy Parker example: " 'Well!' the young man said, 'Well!' she said. 'Well, here we are,' he said. 'Here we are,' she said, 'Aren't we?' 'I should say we were,' he said, 'Eeyop! Here we are.' 'Well!' she said. 'Well!' " Jakobson continues, "The endeavor to start and sustain communication is typical of talking birds; thus the phatic function of language is the only one they share with human beings. It is also the first verbal function acquired by infants; they are prone to communicate before being able to send or receive informative communication." According to my informal survey of young parents, the time a child is most apt to try to sustain conversation is at bedtime, just as the parent has tried to cut it off with "Go to sleep!" As long as this conversation is directed toward the parent (or another person), it would be classified as part of the interactional function. When all hope of communication with someone else is gone, and the child tries to stay awake by talking to himself, it is classified as avoidance (see below).

Personal Function   This function (the "Here I come!" function) as described by Halliday[7] includes expressive or emotive language—language used for the direct expression of feelings and attitudes—but goes beyond this to include the language the child uses "as a form of his own individuality." Halliday[8] says "With the normal child, his awareness of himself is closely bound up with speech: both with hearing himself speak, and with having at his disposal the range of behavioral options that constitute language. Within the concept of the self as an actor, having discretion, or freedom of choice, the 'self as a speaker' is an important component." The child offers to someone else something unique to the child—something he has to say. It is the child's own gift. Through this kind of personal interchange, the child's personality develops.

For example, at 5:9, Greg's mother had asked him to stand still while she combed his hair. He seemed to think he had been standing too long, and said, "I'm beginning to feel very standish." And at 5:5, Greg said, "I finally feel five. For a long time I felt four. Now I know why you have birthdays. When you get too big for your number, you have a birthday." Some children (as well as adults) express their feelings more readily than others.

Long before children have language with which to express feelings, they find nonverbal ways of letting their feelings be known. They smile, laugh, wave their arms happily, reach out for persons they like or pull back from persons they do not know or like. For example, when Brandon was 0:9, a period of ten days elapsed during which he did not see Fred and Leslie, both of whom were favorite friends. On this tenth day, when Leslie came in after school, Brandon squealed, laughed, clapped his hands, and started chattering (babbling) madly. It was perfectly clear that he was delighted to see her, but as yet he had no good way of expressing it verbally. We continue for a lifetime to use some of these clear nonverbal signals for expressing our feelings, and some individuals never rely heavily on language for this.

Children's awareness of themselves as "speakers" is sometimes evident at an early age. For example, Brandon had learned to call Barb *Bar* by 1:6, but when his mother pointed to Barb and said, "Who is that?" Brandon pointed to her and started to say it, then stopped abruptly as his lips were forming the *b* sound. He seemed to be suddenly self-conscious about his voice and a little embarrassed. By about 2:5 Leslie was aware of her difficulty in producing many words and, in addition to practicing them diligently, would often refuse to try to say words, objecting, "I can't. That is hard!" (a combination of personal and metalingual functions).

Heuristic Function   This function is used as a means of exploring the environment, of learning about things, and is typified by "why" questions. Halliday[9] says, "The young child is very well aware of how to use language to learn, and may be quite conscious of this aspect of language before he reaches school; many children already control a metalanguage for the heuristic function of language, in that they know what a 'question' is, what an 'answer' is, what 'knowing' and 'understand-ing' mean, and they can talk about these things without difficulty.'' Mackay and Thompson[10] have shown the importance of helping the child who is learning to read and write to build up a language for talking about language; and it is the heuristic function which provides one of the foundations for this, since the child can readily conceptualize and verbalize the basic categories of the heuristic model. To put this more concretely, the normal five-year-old either already uses words such as *question* and *answer* in their correct meanings or, if he does not, is capable of learning to do so.

Question-asking begins at a very early age, as discussed in Chapter 2. One of the early questions asked is for names of objects. "What dat?" is one of the first questions asked by many children. When the object has previously been named (perhaps a hundred times or more!), one may safely assume that the child is using the question for interactive purposes, but sometimes it is used to obtain information. Questions of many kinds help a child learn about the world. At 1:8 Brandon saw a large button and asked, "Is this butt?" (Is this a button?) His knowledge of buttons had come principally from smaller buttons on his own clothes. And when Brandon was 2:2 I had spent the morning with him, and after I left, Barb said that three or four times during the day, whenever Brandon heard the doorbell or a noise out in front, he asked "Where We?" (Where's Weeks?)

What and *where* questions usually emerge first, and *who, how,* and *why* questions a little later. As with "What dat?" questions, "Why?" questions are often asked routinely, more to keep the speaker's attention than to gather information about the world, but not always, of course.

Language that is used to genuinely search for knowledge may be of the "Tell me about . . ." type or questions such as the following: Greg (5:1) "What does S-A-L-E spell?" He had ridden his Big Wheel car up to the corner and had seen a sign. His mother told him what it spelled, and he said, "Whew. I thought it said 'Don't come up to the corner.' " And Fred (4:4), looking at the waves of San Francisco Bay washing up on shore, "What makes the water so wrinkled?"

It should be mentioned parenthetically here that children can, and often do, explore their environment and find out how things work without asking questions. Leslie, in particular, was a child who asked very few questions in spite of a high level of intelligence. She did most of her exploring by more direct means, such as doing things herself, going places, getting into things, as well as by indirect means, such as starting a conversation on a topic she was interested in and waiting for answers to come forth.

Imaginative Function   This is the language of make-believe, and to the extent that it involves other persons playing with the child, or other persons as listeners, it falls within the classification of a communicative function; in instances where the child is playing alone without regard for others, it may be classified as noncommunicative (and is discussed more fully later in this chapter and in Chapter 3). Children use the imaginative function to expand their own world, to have fun, and to explore possibilities that cannot be explored in the "real" world. This is part of the charm of blocks for children: blocks can become anything the child wishes to think of, such as houses, cars, airplanes, or people. As is indicated in the introduction to Chapter 2, as late as 6:0, John built a "ten thousand story apartment building" with blocks. At the beginning of this chapter, Leslie was using blocks to play house with. She did not explain "This block represents a bed, and this block represents a person sleeping on it." She played with them and talked about them as though these representations were common knowledge between us. Universally, children use materials symbolically in play activities.

In the following example, Leslie and John were given a supply of small toys, including cars, planes, and plastic animals. Perhaps less imagination is required in this case than in the case of using blocks to represent everything, but the child must provide most of the action:

> Leslie (4:6): Excuse me, doggie, doggie.
> John (6:0): I want to . . . Where do you want to go?
> Leslie: I want to go to Disneyland.
> John: Look out! This is also an aircraft carrier. Don't go down there! Don't go down there.
> Leslie: How come?
> John: Because down there's the super . . . All right. No, don't go down there.
> Leslie: Bye bye. See? This is the horse he doesn't live with me. And he makes some. . . . Nobody wants to live with me.

A good deal of action is supplementing the language as the two move across the floor with their toys.

Some children also make up stories as they turn the pages of a book, or upon the request, "Tell me a story." At the beginning of Chapter 3 is a story (of sorts) that Greg was making up as he looked at a book. Of the seven children whose language development I monitor, the five who are old enough to tell a story all have done this upon occasion as they turn the pages of picture books. This activity would seem to be dependent upon having heard stories read to them. A child who has books available but who has seldom if ever had anyone read books to him is not likely to use imaginative language in this way. They may, however, use imaginative language in talking to make-believe persons. For example, Greg (5:3) said, "You know, as I was telling my secret friend, somewhere in the world right now, someone is going to the store." From about 3:0 to 5:0, Fred had an imaginary friend named Jerry, and John's "secret friend" for at least two years was Mr. Mops. He and Mr. Mops shared many adventures. At 4:9 he asked, "Do you know what Mr. Mops' last name is? It's Dab." "Dad?" "No, Dab. D-A-B. Mr. Mops Dab Weeks. And his wife's name is Mrs. Mops Dab Sops." This can be classified as imaginative, but it might also be thought of as poetic to the extent that John is thinking of the sounds of these words and enjoying them. Mops Dab Sops—it *is* a unique sounding name.

The imaginative function is used extensively by preschool children, and is an important one in their development. It is too often the case, however, that the day they enter school, they no longer have any need for this function. Some teachers wisely continue to offer children opportunities to use this function in storytelling, writing, and other activities that encourage the child's unfettered use of language.

Informational Function   Halliday refers to this as the " 'I've got something to tell you' function." It is the expression of propositions, of communicating about something. As Halliday describes it, it is the passing along of information not already known by the listener. When the child points to a picture in a book and says "cat," the child is not communicating new information, and Halliday did not include such comments in this function. It is the passing along of new information that makes this function later in appearing than Halliday's other functions in the child's repertoire of functions. Naming objects, such as described in the naming game in Chapter 3, is used as a means of interacting with other persons, and would be classified as such. Language that *refers* has been called *referential*, or *denotative*, and such speech might qualify for the informational function ("That's a milking stool"), but not necessarily.

The informational function may appear as early as 1:6, before there is much language with which to inform. At this age, Brandon took a rubber ball that had a dog's face on it (and was shaped somewhat like a dog's face, too) over to where Kara (0:8) was sitting in a low chair. He held the doggy-ball in front of her and started his babbling in sentence-like intonation patterns. Every now and then in the babbling, one could identify "oof," which was Brandon's general word for *dog* (he called his own dog, whose name was Daisy, /dayzət/). He gave the appearance of passing along to Kara the information that this was, in fact, a dog. We will never know whether or not Kara received the message, but she was entertained by it all.

An example of Leslie's passing on new information to me follows:

> Leslie (2:11): /i mami bek i vr vi mi/
> Weeks: Mommy's doing what?
> Leslie: /e mami i wi i bwin i . . . i . . . i . . . mek i wes visis/
> Weeks: Mommy's making Jason a Beezie?
> Leslie: /yɛ e bini ə ve bes ʌpar/ "Yes. His Beezie . . . came Jason's apart." (Jason's Beezie, a stuffed clown, came apart.)

Jason was a friend of Leslie's, and her mother had made both of them stuffed clowns that were alike. I was well acquainted with the Beezie clowns but did not know that Leslie's mother was making Jason a new one.

In another instance, I asked for information:

> Weeks: Gregory, tell me what you've been doing.
> Greg (4:5): Well, one thing I've been doing is playing around the playroom.
> Weeks: The playroom? What playroom?
> Greg: The playroom . . . I . . . at the bedroom.
> Weeks: What's the playroom?
> John (8:0): The playroom means Gregory's bedroom. Now we have bunk beds.
> Weeks: Oh, you do? I didn't know that. So you both sleep in the same room now and the other one's a playroom?

We see that in a natural setting, when questions are asked, it is usually[11] because the conversational partner wants to know something he does not already know. In this case, Greg started out giving me new information and John clarified it. In the classroom, on the contrary, the teacher may offer new information to the children, but when the teacher asks questions, she usually expects them to give her information she already has. She is testing the child's knowledge or memory, not asking to be enlightened. For the child, this may be a new function of language, one that is meaningless to him. I have sometimes asked children to tell me their name, as soon as the tape recorder is turned on, so that this information will not be lost. More than once a child has objected, saying, "But you know that." When I was asking for information that the child knew I had, I soon learned to explain why I wanted it. As soon as they understood that there was a reason for repeating known information, they complied. Children may sometimes be puzzled at school to be asked to use language for this purpose. It is not the informational function, and in fact we have no category into which it fits neatly. I am not suggesting that this is not a legitimate use for language, just that it is one that is usually strange to a young child, and that this strangeness is not usually recognized by teachers.

Just as imperative sentences are typical of the instrumental and regulatory functions of language, declarative sentences are typical of the informational function.

Poetic Function The poetic function in children is not used exclusively, or even primarily, for inventing or repeating poetry. Rather it is the use of language in such a way that the user enjoys the sounds. In the introduction to Ruth Weir's *Language in the Crib*,[12] Jakobson made the observation that in adult language, the poetic function and metalingual function were quite separate but in Anthony's bedtime soliloquies, they were intimately interlaced. Young children often repeat utterances because they enjoy the sound, and to the listener, it may appear to be language practice (and perhaps it is). For example, is Anthony practicing, or enjoying sounds in the following?:

"Bobo's not throwing
Bobo can throw
Bobo can throw it
Bobo can throw
Oh oh
Go go go."

Whatever else he is doing, he appears to be enjoying the sound of *o*, and the passage can probably be attributed to both the poetic and metalingual functions.

Sometimes when children invent new words, it can be attributed to the poetic function, also. For a period of at least several months, John (4:0-4:6) used the word *frickly* to mean bumpy, rough, or undesirable in some way. I agree, *frickly* does sound undesirable. And Greg said his grandfather's voice sounded very grampish. These do not seem to be instances in which children are misremembering a word—making a mistake, as when Greg (5:6) called sociology *soshalogity*—but appear to be instances of children having concepts for which they have no words. The words John and Greg invented seem to have a nice ring to them—not onomatopoeic, but suggestive in some way of the meaning intended for the word.

The following example is more nearly what we think of when we use the term poetic language:

> Leslie is playing in the bathtub with a plastic doll and a plastic horse, using a singsong, falsetto voice.
>
> Leslie (6:3): Again I go to France.
>> I go again to France.
>> Fairy I lost my pants.
>> My name is Harry.
>> Some people call me Harry pig toe.
>> My dad, he is Francis.
>> And my love to pants.
>> I used to like my pants,
>> but I don't have any pants
>> because I lost my shirt
>> and Daddy has had a burp,
>> so (she burps) pardon me, that was a burp (she burps again),
>> pardon me, that was a burp.
>> I think I'm wearing my shirt,
>> my black shirt,
>> my black mask,
>> my black pants.
>> And my name is Harry nice,
>> I'm very nice,
>> and father rides.
>> I hate my mice
>> because I am only thrice.
>> That means three.
>
> Weeks: What's the horse's name again?
> Leslie: My name is Harry.

Leslie's singsong voice and pauses indicated that this was in the nature of a song or poem, rather than simple role playing, and the nonsensical nature of the language reinforces this interpretation.

It might be argued convincingly that this language was noncommunicative and should be classed as language play, but I was sitting right beside the bathtub with the microphone, and Leslie directed some of her speech to me from time to time. She alternately spoke for the horse and for the doll, using a somewhat different sound for each of them, and even when I asked for the horse's name, she continued to play the role of the horse as she answered "My name is Harry." Whether her language was communicative or not, it was definitely poetic. Words such as *thrice* seemed to have been chosen specifically because they rhymed. *Burp* is also a near-rhyming word for *shirt* and may have been chosen the first time for that reason. It should be mentioned here that such unrestrained use of language gives children a chance to use words such as *thrice* which are in their vocabulary but for which the child has no ordinary use. We can easily see that adults who respond to such language with "Oh, don't be silly!" or something similar may dampen the child's language development.

Personality characteristics, rather than linguistic skill, seem to determine children's use of the poetic function, as well as other aspects of language development and use. For example, Fred and John were both willing to use new words and take a chance on using them somewhat inappropriately sometimes. Leslie was not, but would occasionally use out-of-the-ordinary vocabulary items such as *thrice* in a playful way where she had no chance of being embarrassed.

Jakobson[13] offers other examples of arranging language for sound, such as the ordering of names in one way rather than another. We may always say *Joan and Margery,* but never *Margery and Joan,* or *Jim and Alice,* but never *Alice and Jim.* Jakobson reports that the person using *Joan and Margery* (twins) said "It sounds smoother." Writers of good advertising copy and slogans make use of this poetic function regularly without actually writing poetry. Many children also make extensive use of it, while others use it much less. It is discussed further in Chapter 3.

Interpretive Function   Tough[14] has proposed the interpretive function and the projective functions. Her interpretive function "relates to immediate and recalled experiences and is concerned with organizing the experience at different levels of meaning." This would include reasoning, the recognition of causes and effects, recognizing sequence, and abstraction of central meaning. These reflect the child's attempt to find meaning in his experiences. Tough's projective functions include three facets: predictive, imaginative, and empathetic. The predictive (predictably) predicts. It includes the anticipation of consequences, prediction of solutions, recognition of problems, and in general, thinking beyond the actual present or recalled experience. I am including this in the interpretive function. The imaginative function has already been discussed and is not included here. The empathetic function is one in which the child projects into the feelings and lives of others. This is included here in the interpretive function, except where it might be a part of the imaginative function.

Children under two or three years of age will rarely be noted using the interpretive function, but beyond age three or four, it becomes common. The earliest example I have that may be considered interpretive occurred when Barb was holding Kara as she asked Brandon, "Do you have a dirty diaper?" Brandon immediately poked Kara's bottom and said "Does!" Barb called it passing the buck, for it was Brandon who was the guilty party, but I call it the use of the interpretive function. It surely is not informational (and we do not presently have a function called misinformational!), for Brandon knew perfectly well the facts in the case, and was misrepresenting them! Or should it be classified as imaginative?

In the following example, at age 3:0, Leslie used both the informational and interpretive functions:

> Leslie: I /æ/ one more /e/ Daddy /ʌ/ me. (I have one more
> (book) that Daddy gave me.)
> Fred: Daddy didn't give you a book, Leslie!
> Leslie (looking at Fred): /ɛð/ he do. That one. Daddy /e/
> me. (Yes, he did. That one, Daddy gave me.)
> Leslie (looking at me): Fwed /ɪ nɑwi/ (Fred is naughty.)

Leslie gave me information that I did not already have—that her father had given her a book (informational function) and then interpreted Fred's behavior in disagreeing with her as being naughty (interpretive function). If she had looked at Fred and scolded him with "You're naughty!" it would have been classified as the use of the personal function, but in this case, she appeared to be offering me an explanation for Fred's remark.

Again Leslie combined the informational and interpretive functions, this time at age 4:7, as she was looking at pictures of cowboys and their horses at a rodeo.

> Leslie: One horse is licking somebody. Cause he likes
> 'em. . . . That cowboy and ah they have cowboy hats on.
> And they are mean.

Weeks: Are they mean?

Leslie: Yeah. Lots a cowboys are mean and they don't like
anybody. And the horses are mad at them and tryin' to
get over them . . . and trying to get . . . try to dump them
on them . . . like their people and their horses.

Such a segment of speech combines the informational function (making
comments on the picture) and the interpretive function (interpreting the
actions and feelings of both the horse and the men).

In this example, Jennie (3:2) was interpreting the behavior of another
animal, a cat. She was in a store looking at a poster of a cat with its
mouth wide open. First she said rather softly, "That Walter" (the name
of their cat), then added, a little more loudly, "That Walter 'creaming."
As she continued to look at the poster, it became more vivid in her mind
that the cat was in trouble, and she said, very loudly, "He 'creaming
HELP! HELP! HELP!" By the third *help*, she was almost screaming
herself, and people were beginning to stare.

As mentioned above, the interpretive function also includes reminisc-
ing about past events, placing values and meaning on them. In the
following exchange, John and Greg recall happy experiences in snow
country:

Greg (4:5): The snow was really fun because . . . um . . . me
and Zoe, we went in the deep snow, and um . . .

John (8:0) (interrupting): . . . deep snow was about as high
as . . .

Greg: . . . and um, and ah, when we moved, when we, ah, in
Michigan also, there was a real little path, real pathway to
get in to go through our door.

Weeks: Did you? Pathway from where?

John: From the xxx . . . (I didn't understand his answer.)

Greg: Yeah.

Weeks: From where?

John: When they started building construction, I liked it. I
liked it before that too, cause we ah . . . we would always
play on dirt hills. They were hills made out of dirt.

Weeks: So the pathway was from where, Gregory?

Greg: Um, from the, from the driveway.

Memories may be recalled without the use of oral language,
interpretations may be placed on the behavior of other persons or

animals, the sequence of events may be recognized, causes and effects may be deduced, all without language. There is no claim here that language is essential for these functions, only that language may be used for these functions. It is also interesting that the verbalization of such experiences of interpretations helps the recall of that experience at a later time. We all have had the experience of remembering what we *said* about an event without actually remembering the event. We still have much to learn about the role language plays, but we know it is a vital one.

Performative Function   This function includes such language as promises, bets, and curses, and comprises a very small proportion of the total output of a child's language. In the strictest sense of the term,[15] the performative function is one that is not used often even by adults. When a minister says "I pronounce you man and wife," or an umpire says "You're out!" or a judge says "You're guilty!" they are using the performative function to do something with words. The nonministers, nonumpires, and nonjudges among us cannot perform such acts with words, but we can make promises, bets, etc. Most of us would agree that for children this is a rather insignificant function, but it is one which should be recognized.

I have recorded no bets in the speech of the seven children I observe, and the promises (and threats) are usually directed to dolls or stuffed animals: "I'm putting you in the corner, cuz you're naughty!" John was heard several times from about 5:0 to 8:0 promising to bring a surprise of some kind home to Greg, but without using the word *promise*: "I'll bring you something, Greg!" Inasmuch as he did, in fact, bring something back, it may be assumed that he meant it as a promise, and certainly Greg understood it that way.

I have not recorded Greg actually making any promises, but at 5:5, he commented "I threw away my promise," meaning that he did not intend to keep it (you throw away things you don't want to keep).

Noncommunicative Functions of Language

Language that we direct to ourselves is no less important in our lives than the language directed to others. Small children may say everything they think about (Piaget[16] says "He says everything. He has no verbal continence"), but by the time children are school-age, and perhaps much, much younger, they are able to think with language. Some of the noncommunicative speech used by children is similar to that used by ourselves when we are under stress and we revert to talking to ourselves,

Table 2   Noncommunicative Functions of Language

Name of function	How child uses it	Examples from child speech
1. Language play	Amuses one's self; creates interesting language patterns	bink ben bink, blue kink
2. Metalingual (language practice)*	Repeats language segments as though "practicing" language, talks about language	bag[h] bukth (Adult: Box?) bak bak bak∫
3. Concept formation	Uses language as an aid to forming concepts	(trying to decide what color something is) Black. Kinda blueth (bluish). Blackshish
4. Self-directing (directive, private speech, egocentric speech)	Uses language to control and direct one's own behavior	This paper gonna be good all right. I think I gonna cut it
5. Self-image formation	Private speech that functions to define the child's roles and self-image	(decorating cookies) Arrow. I'm doing a good job
6. Avoidance	Uses speech to avoid something worse, such as sleep	ba ba rattit ba ba rattit
7. Magical	Considers words to have qualities or powers in themselves	No, Greg. Cat. Our cat

*Terms enclosed in parentheses are those used by other writers for the same or a similar function.

but much of it is uniquely childlike. Table 2 lists the noncommunicative functions of child language, explains briefly how the child uses it, and offers some examples.

Language Play   Language that qualifies for this category is that which is used solely for the child's own enjoyment. Language play can also be used for social purposes, and is discussed more fully in Chapter 3. Examples such as the telephone conversations recorded between two young children by Ervin-Tripp and Mitchell-Kernan[17] and Keenan's report[18] of her twin sons demonstrate clearly that language play can be communicative, and as such could be categorized as the interactional or imaginative functions. However, it is perhaps more usual for children's language play to be indulged in for self-entertainment purposes. For example, Gregory made up a poem pattern which he fleshed out in various ways and used apparently for his own enjoyment: "Dad, dad, stick and stad," "Zoe, Zoe, stick and sto-ey," etc. He said it in a singsong voice as he went about the house, and did not seem to expect anyone to notice or respond. Many nice examples are also found in Weir's[19] description of Anthony's bedtime soliloquies. Since Weir used a hidden voice-activated microphone, and no one else was in the room when Anthony was talking, one can feel very confident that Anthony's speech was noncommunicative. When a child produces similar language, say, for example, the poem/song that Leslie produced while playing in the bathtub, with another person nearby and attending to what the child is saying, and with the child directing language to that other person from time to time, one cannot feel comfortably certain about the communicative nature of the language, from the child's point of view. Because Leslie looked at me from time to time and smiled, perhaps checking to see if I was continuing to pay attention to her, I have categorized the passage just mentioned as communicative, much as I did Jennie's monologue discussed in Chapter 2.

Sound effects that children produce as they play can usually be categorized as language play also. At 1:11, for example, Brandon never seemed to push a car or toy across the floor without supplying some noises that might be interpreted as motor noises. When Brandon played, all mechanical toys made mechanical noises, and animals made a variety of sounds. Such sounds appeared to be entirely for his own enjoyment. Sometimes when children are required to be quiet during such play, the activity simply stops, because the sounds seem to be an essential part of the play.

Metalingual To the listener, language play and language practice may sound identical. The child may repeat sounds, as in babbling, or may repeat words, intonation patterns, as Jennie did (discussed in Chapter 3), sentence patterns, or strings of sentences. The difference lies in the child's intentions: is the child entertaining himself or treating language as one might if one were learning a second language? Some children also begin to talk about language at fairly early ages. Language that talks about language is called metalanguage, and both Weir[20] and Jakobson[21] refer to it as such, in reference to child language.

Jakobson[22] also points out that language is performing a metalingual (that is, glossing) function when a person asks, "I don't follow you—what do you mean?" Attention is focused on the *code* (the symbols for meaning). Are the two speakers using the same code? Do *sophisticated* and *sophomore* mean the same to the speaker as they do to the hearer? In much the same way, a child focuses on the code in practicing language. For example, when Leslie said "yeth" and I asked "dress?" I was asking, "When you say *yeth* do you mean the same thing I mean when I say *dress*?" Her ensuing practicing was for the purpose of making the language she already had more similar to mine. Jakobson also suggests that "Any process of language learning, in particular child acquisition of the mother tongue, makes wide use of such metalingual operations; and aphasia may often be defined as a loss of ability for metalingual operations." Use of language to improve one's language in some way, to talk about language, or to focus on the code is considered here to be a function of child language—the metalingual function.

When a child indulges in such exercises as the following, it seems as though he is practicing:[23]

> One two three four
> One two
> One two three four
> One two three
> Anthony counting
> Good boy you
> One two three
> Here the child even informs us what he is doing, he commends himself for the activity and counts once more for good measure. He not only produces the speech event, but discusses it as well, as if he were citing someone else. It is very doubtful that he fully understands the concept of numbers. He is learning to count as a linguistic activity, and yet usually the numbers appear in ascending order as in the example, with one culminating line.

Perhaps Anthony was just having fun with language, for language acquisition was relatively easy for him. In examining the transcripts of recordings of Fred's speech, I found no examples of speech that sounded like language practice, and Halliday[24] commented that Nigel did very little language practicing. There are hundreds of examples of Leslie practicing language, however. She practiced word pronunciations more than anything else. At 2:7, she was referring to a dress and called it "a yeth." I wasn't certain what she meant, and asked, "A dress?" Then, having a model to work from, she practiced: "defth . . . deth . . . dwesh," producing the initial consonant correctly each time, even though the final consonant was not (the vowel was correct in all instances). At 2:11, Leslie had gotten out her viewfinder and wanted us to look at some pictures in it:

> Weeks: Oh, all right. Shall we look at the pictures now?
> Leslie: No. /ɪ mɪtɪt jɛrt pɪʃurz/ (No. In a minute. ? Pictures.)
> Weeks: Oh, Peter Pan. These are the pictures and a little story.
> Leslie: Yeah, these are /bɪtdrž/. These a /bɪsrs/. (Yeah, these are pictures. These are pictures.)

Each trial was a little different, but she was practicing, trying to improve her production of the word. Leslie appeared to be aware of the difficulty she had in acquiring the sound system of the language and worked diligently at it.[25] Most children probably fall somewhere in between Fred and Leslie in the amount of language practice they indulge in.

Children also talk *about* language. Goodman[26] told of a little boy who called some cookies "the goodest" he had ever eaten. His mother informed him that there was no such word as *goodest*. Thoughtful pause. "Then how come I can say it?"

I discovered that by the time John was 4:9, he was able to discuss some aspects of his knowledge of English, even though he was handicapped by lack of vocabulary in discussing certain grammatical aspects. By this age children are using a great many suffixes (such as *-ish* or *-able*) productively, often in nonadult ways, and I was interested to see to what extent a child could talk about such word endings. One suffix that I asked John about was the diminutive ending *-ie* or *-y*. I asked "What would it mean if you said *horse* and *horsie*?" Without hesitation, he explained, "A *horsie* is a baby horse. Means the same thing as a *dog* and a *doggy*. For every animal it means the same thing. Right? Whenever you say a *pup* or a *puppy* or a *giraffe* and *giraffie*, it would be the same thing." Just to be sure, I asked, "Now, what would a *giraffie* be?" He said, "It would be a small giraffe." John was also willing to go on and apply the same principle to inanimate objects. I asked, "Are there any other words that you can think of that you could add an /i/ to make them like a baby?" He quickly supplied "*Pillowie* and *pillow*." I asked, "How about *chair* and *chairie*?" "Well," he said, "a *chairie* would be just like a little rocking chair, or something, and a *chair* would be just a plain old chair." Although not all native speakers of English will agree with

John about the meaning of the diminutive suffix, it can be seen that he had drawn some conclusions about its function, and was willing and able to discuss it. The metalingual function was well established at 4:9, and undoubtedly earlier, but I had not asked the questions needed at an earlier time to determine its development.

Concept Formation   In the everyday sense, a concept is a thought or an idea; in logic it is more specifically an idea comprehending the essential attributes of a class of logical species. For example, when a child learns to differentiate between apples and pears, or between dogs and horses, he is forming a "concept of apples" or of pears, or of dogs or horses. As Rees[27] has pointed out, "the major achievement of conceptualizing appears to be that it enables the organism to minimize the complexity of his environment. A stock of concepts against which to match environment stimuli permits the developing organism to address his attention to relevant features and ignore irrelevant ones, thus reducing 'cognitive load.' "

Some psychologists have maintained that concepts are formed independent of language learning and that naming, or labeling, by a child is merely an indication that the conceptualization has taken place. A different view is taken by those who believe that language facilitates the formation of concepts: the child responds to an unfamiliar word as an indication that there is a category to be acquired. The child then proceeds to classify the objects seen according to the words he has already learned. For example, at 1:7, Brandon had learned the word *cow*, and had learned it well enough that he could always identify a real cow or picture of a cow correctly. When he was shown a picture of a camel, he pointed and said "cow." He was told, "It's a camel. It looks a little bit like a cow, but it's not. It's a camel." Brandon pointed again and said "Cow!" "No, it's a camel." "Cow!!" Having acquired a new category, he did not want to be confused by the facts! Children are almost invariably reported to include within a newly acquired category some objects that do not belong there. In this instance, Brandon was apparently basing his classification on some visual aspect of cows and camels, and most cases reported at this age are similar to this. Less usual is the following case, in which Brandon makes his judgment based on the name, despite dissimilar appearance:

Brandon (1:9) (taking the microphone from my hand and holding it out toward me): This is? (What is this?)
Weeks: A microphone.

(Brandon immediately put the microphone against his neck
and raised his shoulder, cradling the microphone as
though he were holding a telephone receiver on his
shoulder. He smiled and started babbling softly as he
always does when talking on his toy telephone. Twice
within an hour, he used the microphone again this way.)

The classification here of a microphone as a telephone was apparently
based on his attending to *phone* in *microphone*. There was little, if any,
physical similarity between the microphone and a telephone; his toy
telephone is pink; the real telephones Brandon sees are ivory wall phones.
He may, however, have deduced that both objects had something to do
with talking, but he had never used the microphone as a telephone before
I told him the name of it. In this instance, Brandon was led astray by
using the name as a basis for categorization, but it indicates that children
do use language to help in concept formation.

The television program, Sesame Street, regularly uses exercises to help
their viewers with concept formation. One of their methods is to ask
"Are these the same or different?" By age 3:2, Leslie had watched
Sesame Street many times, and often asked herself this question:

Leslie (playing with colored blocks and talking to herself):
These same? Not. No, one's a little wider. Uh, /e/ not uh
same. One belongs green. One belongs blue.

After listening repeatedly to children put themselves through such
exercises, it is impossible not to believe that language is vital in concept
formation.

Werner and Kaplan[28] take an extreme view of maintaining that the
process of naming, or symbolizing, *is* the process of concept formation.
There is a wide divergence of opinions about the precise role that
language plays in concept formation, but most psychologists believe that
language plays a significant role, and that is the view taken here.

Self-Directing   This function, sometimes referred to simply as the
directive function, refers to language that directs one's own actions. It is
heard as children are engaged in play activities of all kinds such as Leslie
talking about the blue and green blocks above. At early ages, talk may
merely accompany play activities, but by the time children are beyond
the earliest language-acquisition stages, language becomes a tool in
helping the child solve problems encountered in play. For example,

Tough[29] offers the following example of a three-year-old girl, Linda, who is playing dolls:

> (Linda talks quietly to herself. Her voice is almost a monotone. She puts the doll into bed—and looks around.)
> Linda: Putting her to bed. In the bed. Like that. Puts legs down. Now . . .
> (Linda speaks loudly and more clearly, but is not addressing anyone. Her speech just anticipates her action as she turns to the box and turns over the contents. She returns to the bed, and gradually her voice fades away.)
> Linda: . . . well . . . a cover. Where's a cover? I'll have to find a cover . . . in the box . . . here . . . that'll do for a cover . . . there . . . put round . . . make you warm . . . There . . . that's nice and warm baby.

Linda's speech at first appears to be merely monitoring her actions, but later seems to be directing herself in finding a solution. Language helps focus the child's attention on the action.

Anyone who has observed children playing with cars, drawing, building with blocks, or in similar activities has heard the talk that goes along with the action. This speech is not directed to anyone else (though Vygotsky finds it diminishes when there is no listener present), and children do not expect an answer to questions such as "Where's a cover?" Even such remarks as "See? I'm almost finished!" are often directed to one's self. Such language helps the child monitor, direct, and plan his own actions.

Self-Image Formation   Long before children have anything resembling a formal language system, they have begun to form an image of themselves. As with other language functions, language is not the only means of forming self-image, but it is a powerful means. Psychologists and our common sense tell us that children who repeatedly hear comments such as "You're a mean little kid!" "You're so slow!" or "Why are you always so messy!" will probably grow up thinking of themselves as mean, slow, or messy. Children take cues from speech directed to them to direct speech to themselves, in the function of self-image formation. Some schoolteachers, particularly at kindergarten and primary-grade levels, evaluate students, along with reading and math, on their self-image. An evaluation might say (in part), "John has an excellent self-image." Children learn to assess this in themselves as they get older. For example, when Fred was in the sixth grade, I asked him about his teacher and he reported, "She's sarcastic. No one has a very good self-image by the time they've been in her class for a year."

The building of self-image is abetted, however, by children's own language directed to themselves. In the following example, Leslie seemed to be trying to build up an image of herself as a brave child:

> Leslie (2:11) (looking at pictures and talking to herself): /e bɛ... i bɛg hurt mi³⁰ ... e o mi/ (Lady bug. Lady bug won't hurt me. They love me.)
> /e wurn... e wurn i kɛr mi... e o mi/ (A worm. A worm doesn't scare me. They love me.)

This pattern was repeated with caterpillars, a lion, a horse, a mouse, and a rooster. As she turned the pages of the picture book, she kept reminding herself that the animals and insects did not scare her, perhaps because they all loved her. I assume that the pictures were somewhat frightening to her.

In my data, peppered throughout with self-directing speech, are remarks such as "I'm doing a good job," "It's hard, but I can do it," and "I'm a good mommy." Such language is thought to play an important role in a child's self-concept development.

Avoidance   Robinson[31] refers to this function, as applied to adults, as the avoidance of worse activity, the everyday name of which is verbal escapism. The office worker who visits with a coworker because it is preferable to working is typical of the adult use of verbal escapism. The chatter so often encountered at bedtime is most typical of children's use of language to avoid something worse—sleep, but it is certainly not the only time children use it. Another example is when children have been told to pick up their toys, or some other dreaded task, and they begin an animated conversation in an attempt to get their parent to forget the task. That it is seldom a successful ploy does not hinder them from trying it again and again. This is a case where the entire context of the situation must be considered in analyzing the data.

Avoidance of punishment is another motivation for talk. For example, at 1:1 Brandon climbed up on the dining-room table in spite of the fact he knew he was not supposed to climb up on the furniture. When his mother noticed him there, he instantly turned on the charm, chattered gaily, and smiled. The babbling continued at a rapid-fire pace until he saw his mother was merely going to remove him, not punish him. In this case, he made eye contact as he babbled and smiled. In other instances where he knows he has done something he shouldn't, he remained silent and refused to make eye contact, as though he could not be scolded unless he looked at his caretaker.

Magical   In discussing the inspiration for some of his books, Fleischman[32] reported,

> Folklore once again provided me with the basic idea for *Longbeard the Wizard* (Atlantic-Little), a picture book. I was reading a museum-published biography for an exhibit of the paintings of Chaim Soutine. A sentence leaped out at me. Soutine was affected by a folk belief that we are born to speak a certain and unknown number of words; when we use them up, we die. An irresistible idea. Enter Queen Gibble-Gabble, unaware that she is chattering her way into a sudden grave. Trivia? I think not. The magic power of words runs through all cultures.

The belief in the magic power of words seems to start at a very early age, and is much more apparent in some children than in others. Rees[33] suggests that word magic appears to originate from two properties of children's early utterances, "the phenomena known as symbol realism and words-as-actions. The force behind the development of the magical attitude towards words derives from the individual's need to control or manipulate himself and his environment. Symbol realism occurs when words or names are treated as if they are essentially objects in themselves." Brown[34] commented on the tendency of children to behave as though words were inextricably bound to the objects they name, becoming uneasy at the suggestion that anything be called by a name other than the one they know. In Chapter 3, there is an example of Greg's calling their cat a giraffe, and of Jennie becoming upset about it, and correcting him, "No, Greg. Cat. Our cat."

Vygotsky[35] also writes that "the name, once discovered by the child, enters into the structure of the object." The child does not discover that there is a relationship between the name (or sign) and the object or referent, but the name appears to the child to be an attribute of the object or person. If this is the case, it has implications for early child bilingualism. That is, if a child discovers at a very early age that the furry, four-legged animal running around the house may be called either a *dog* or *chien*, is the child learning at an early age that labels are not an inherent property of the animal, or does it merely suggest that there are alternatives, such as referring to the pet as *dog, puppy,* or *Rover?* Evidence to date suggests that knowing two languages may free a child from the tyranny of words, but research is scant.

Experiences with taboo words (for example, "Don't you ever say _____ again!") may also reinforce a child's notion that at least some words have magical powers. The power of curses may also be related to this function. The magical function may be as important in adult language as in child language. It is probably reflected in the use of euphemisms and the avoidance of certain words, and as Fleischman points out, it is found in all cultures.

Discussion

Developmental Order   In a careful study of the language functions of one child, Nigel, Halliday[36] found developmental order, namely, that the first four functions to emerge almost simultaneously at 0:9 to 0:10½ are instrumental, regulatory, interactional, and personal. The next three to emerge are heuristic and imaginative at 1:1 to 1:3, and informational (all Halliday's terms) at 1:9 to 1:10½. Halliday suggests that the only model of language that many adults have is the informational one ("I have something to tell you") but that this is a very inadequate model for the child and is not acquired at an early age. That is, children do not have new information to offer at an early age—during most of the first two years they use language almost exclusively for other purposes. As may be seen by the ages listed, these functions proposed by Halliday are for children up to about two years old. I know of no systematic research on the age or order of acquisition of the other functions listed in Tables 1 or 2, but for children up to about age eight, the performative function may be expected to be among the last to appear.

Of noncommunicative functions, language play is usually first to appear. The order of the acquisition of the others is not known and in any event may be expected to vary with individual children to some extent.

Adult versus Child Functions   Halliday[37] has suggested that it is sometimes the case that the teacher's image of language is narrower and less rich than that which is already present in the minds of the children. The teacher may have long since stopped using imaginative or poetic language, for example, and may expect the child to use little except the informational function in the classroom. However, there is sometimes a problem of the opposite kind. Adults often use language figuratively, while children seldom do. For example, Mackay and Thompson told about a little girl who thought she must be deaf because she was unable to hear any noise at all when her teacher asked her "What does this letter say?" The little girl couldn't hear the letter whispering, and she reported feeling a great relief when she was eight years old and discovered that letters don't really say anything. This is a common figure of speech, and is not the same as language play. Adults are not pretending that a letter is really talking when they refer to the letter saying certain sounds, in the way a child is pretending his teddy bear is talking. There are countless examples of the confusion of children over figurative speech. Children are inclined to interpret language literally, in spite of their play with language.

The Sociolinguistic Importance of Functions   It has been noted by many concerned educators and researchers that children from middle-class homes are generally more successful in school than children from lower-class homes. This remains the case even when groups of children are matched for intelligence. It is not much help to point out that schools are largely designed and run by the middle class for middle-class children, for even the most skilled and sympathetic teacher from a lower-class background finds the middle-class children more successful than the lower-class children. The question that has been asked frequently in recent years is: In what way is the language of the child from a lower-class home different from that of the child from a middle-class home? This is vital because language is the umbrella under which all subjects in school cluster; even a subject such as arithmetic is taught by means of language. A child whose comprehension and production of the language of the classroom is insufficient in any way may be expected to suffer scholastically.

Britisher Joan Tough[38] set out to see if the language acquired by children of working-class parents might be different in specifiable ways from the language of children with professional parents. Her research has provided some interesting results.

Her project was a longitudinal study in Leeds, England, of sixty-four children, thirty-two of whom had entered nursery schools or classes at the time of selection at age 3 to 3½, and thirty-two of whom were not expected to have a nursery education because of lack of space in nursery-school programs. These children were seen again in school at the age of 5½ to 7½ years.

The children were drawn from two sections of the population, children from homes where parents were in professions, and homes where parents were unskilled or semiskilled workers. Because these populations were, in relation to one another, at advantage or disadvantage within education, she called the groups *advantaged* and *disadvantaged*, but stressed that these terms were used in relation to education only. The children were all given the Stanford Binet Scale of Intelligence (1960 revision), and were included in the study only if their IQ was 105 or above. Also, no child was included if there were more than six children in the family or if there was any indication of particular stress in the home. As further precaution, only children whose mothers were native speakers of British English were selected, so as to eliminate the possibility that a child's use of a nonstandard dialect could cause problems of misunderstanding. In addition, only children who were speaking clearly at age 3, and who did not seem withdrawn or hostile to the observer, were selected. (These essential precautions had the effect of eliminating the most severely disadvantaged children and make her results more impressive.)

A sampling of the children's language at age 3 consisted of a tape recording of an hour of talk in a play situation. The toys she provided included small cars and a fire engine and a family of small dolls with furniture and house play accessories, including a telephone. The atmosphere was informal; the observer made no effort to stimulate play or conversation but gave support and encouragement to the children as they played.

In view of the present discussion of the role of functions of language for the young child, the following findings regarding the language of Tough's three-year-old group is of exceptional interest:[39]

1 The disadvantaged groups of children used speech two and a half times as often as the advantaged groups to secure attention to their own needs and to maintain their own status by defending or asserting themselves in the face of the needs and actions of others.

2 The advantaged groups used language more than five times as often as the less favored groups for extending or promoting action, and for securing collaboration with others: language is seen to play a directing or controlling role more frequently. The disadvantaged groups used language more often as part of, or as a support to, ongoing action: language tended to accompany action rather than to control or direct it.

3 The advantaged groups used language almost eight times as

often to refer to past experiences and more than twice as often to contemplate the future.

4 The advantaged groups used language more than nine times as frequently for reasoning—in real or imagined contexts. The advantaged groups used more than twice as much speech for projection through the imagination as the disadvantaged groups, and more than five times as much for projecting beyond the use of concrete materials for creating an imagined situation.

5 We attempted to distinguish between language that seemed to require no listener other than the self and that addressed to other children or to the adult. The disadvantaged groups used slightly more speech that appeared to be only for the self than the advantaged groups (17 and 13.6 per cent of all speech respectively). The advantaged groups, on the other hand, addressed the adult more frequently than the disadvantaged groups (30.0 and 19.9 per cent of all utterances respectively). There were differences here between the nursery and the non-nursery groups. The advantaged non-nursery group addressed the adult almost twice as often as the nursery advantaged group (41.2 and 21.1 per cent of all utterances) and, contrary to expectations, the disadvantaged non-nursery group addressed the adult more frequently than the disadvantaged nursery group (23.0 and 15.6 per cent of all utterances).

There is a clear correlation between social class and language function. The difference is not due to a difference in intelligence between the two groups (advantaged and disadvantaged) but is due to the kinds of experience the two groups of children have had with language. It is easy to see how a child whose parents give orders without reasons ("You do it because I told you to!" using a regulatory function) and a child whose parents offer reasons for instructions ("Don't do it because the point is sharp and you may get hurt," using regulatory plus interpretive) may use language very differently in similar situations. Whether or not the child is considered an appropriate conversation partner by the parents will also have lasting effects on the child's ability to use certain kinds of language (see Chapter 2).

This study suggests a promising area for future research in the pragmatics of language.

The Relationship between Form and Function   Rather than looking at the relationship between language function and social class, M. A. K. Halliday has been interested in the relationship between function and grammatical structure. He has noted, for example, that the instrumental and regulatory functions make extensive use of imperatives ("Give me that!" and "Do that right now!"), that the informational function ordinarily makes use of declarative sentences ("I have a new book"), and that the heuristic makes use of questions ("Why do you have freckles?"). Such rules cannot hold for every utterance in any given function. For example, as discussed in Chapter 2, children learn while very young to give orders in nondirect ways; for example, "Shall we wipe a face?" rather than "Wipe my face!" (using a question instead of an imperative, though the two sentences serve the same purpose). Nevertheless, such generalizations are valid as rules of thumb. It is also the case that when children use certain functions, such as the imaginative, they are much more apt to use more complex sentence structures and a wider range of vocabulary items than when using other functions, such as regulatory. If one is gathering a sample of a child's speech for the purpose of calculating the mean length of utterance (MLU), it will be seen that the MLU will be higher if the child is making up a story or role playing, etc., than if the child is playing with blocks or cars. (If one complicates this with an age factor—the child tells a story to an adult in the first case and plays cars with a younger child in the second case—the difference in MLU is even greater.) Certain situations call for certain functions to be put to use, and in turn, for certain linguistic structures to be used in preference to others. Such differences need to be borne in mind in gathering data from children.

Summary

We are born to talk. Under normal conditions, every child learns to speak the language (or languages) of his environment. Children do not set about to learn sentence structures or words; they set about to do things with language, and in this sense, function precedes form (or language structure).

While there is not general agreement on the classification of language functions used by children, there is agreement that they fall into two general categories: communicative and noncommunicative (referred to as socialized and egocentric by Piaget). I have concluded, after reviewing the literature (principally British) and my own data, that the following functions are likely to include all the uses made by children of their language:

Communicative functions
1. Instrumental
2. Regulatory
3. Interactional
4. Personal
5. Heuristic
6. Imaginative
7. Informational
8. Poetic
9. Interpretive
10. Performative

Noncommunicative functions
1. Language play
2. Metalingual
3. Concept formation
4. Self-directing
5. Self-image formation
6. Avoidance
7. Magical

Halliday found developmental order in the first seven communicative functions; they were acquired in the order listed. He has also found a correlation between functions and certain grammatical structures.

In looking for the causes for the differences in school success of middle-class and lower-class children, Joan Tough conducted a longitudinal study of the speech of "advantaged" children (those whose parents held professional positions) and "disadvantaged" children (those whose parents were unskilled or semiskilled workers). Her results indicated (in part) that the disadvantaged children used instrumental and regulatory functions two and a half times as often as the advantaged groups; the advantaged group used interpretive language eight times as often as the disadvantaged; and the advantaged group addressed adults more often than the disadvantaged. The implications of these findings for education are far-reaching.

NOTES

1. Noam Chomsky has attempted to study language as an abstract entity, entirely removed from usage, and maintains that communication is not the basic function of language. Readers interested in pursuing this lively linguistic debate may read: Noam Chomsky, *Syntactic Structures,* The Hague: Mouton, 1957; *Aspects of the Theory of Syntax,* Cambridge, Mass.: MIT Press, 1965; *Language and Mind,* New York: Harcourt Brace Jovanovich, 1972; *Reflections on Language,*

New York: Random House, 1975; Carol F. Feldman, "Two Functions of Language," *Harvard Educational Review*, 1977, 47:282-293; and John Searle, "What Is a Speech Act?" in *The Philosophy of Language*, edited by John R. Searle, London: Oxford University Press, 1971.

2. Halliday, Michael A. K. *Explorations in the Functions of Language*, London: Edward Arnold Publishers, 1973, p. 8.

3. Piaget, Jean. *The Language and Thought of the Child*, New York: Meridian Books, 1955.

4. Discussed further in Chapter 2.

5. *Op. cit.*, p. 13.

6. Jakobson, Roman. "Closing Statement: Linguistics and Poetics," in *Style in Language*, edited by Thomas A. Sebeok, Cambridge, Mass.: MIT Press, 1960, pp. 355-356. The two terms Jakobson used for the interactional function are *contact* and *phatic*.

7. *Op. cit.*

8. *Ibid.*, p. 14.

9. *Ibid.*, p. 15.

10. Mackay, David, and Brian Thompson. *Programme in Linguistics and English Teaching, Paper 3: The Initial Teaching of Reading and Writing*, London: Longmans Green, 1968.

11. Not always, of course. As pointed out in Chapter 2, sometimes questions are asked just to keep a conversation going even though the speaker does not care about the answer.

12. Weir, Ruth Hirsch. *Language in the Crib*, The Hague: Mouton, 1962.

13. Jakobson, Roman. "Closing Statement: Linguistics and Poetics," in *Style in Language*, edited by Thomas A. Sebeok, Cambridge, Mass.: MIT Press, 1960.

14. Tough, Joan. "Children's Use of Language," *Educational Review*, 1974, 26 (iii):166-179, p. 176.

15. Taking it to an extreme point of view, J. L. Austin (*How to Do Things with Words*, New York: Oxford University Press, 1962) points out how virtually every English verb can be considered a performative verb. For example, when a judge says "Guilty!" this is classified by Austin, reasonably enough, as a verdictive, but a verdictive may also consist of the delivery of an unofficial finding, such as "I should call him industrious." The other performatives isolated by Austin are exercitives, commissives, behavitives, and expositives. While this constitutes an interesting intellectual exercise, only the obvious performatives will be considered as such in this book.

16. *The Language and Thought of the Child*, p. 59.

17. Ervin-Tripp, Susan M., and Claudia Mitchell-Kernan (eds.), *Child Discourse*, New York: Academic Press, 1977.

18. Keenan, Elinor O. "Conversational Competence in Children," *Journal of Child Language*, 1974, 1:163-183.

19. *Language in the Crib*.

20. *Ibid.*

21. "Closing Statement: Linguistics and Poetics."

22. *Ibid.*, p. 356.

23. *Language in the Crib*, p. 112.

24. Halliday, Michael A. K. *Learning How to Mean—Explorations in the Development of Language*, London: Edward Arnold Publishers, 1975.

25. Weeks, Thelma E. *The Slow Speech Development of a Bright Child*, Lexington, Mass.: Lexington Books, D.C. Heath, 1974.

26. Goodman, Yetta. "What Should Teachers Do—Implications for Integrating," Panel Presentation for Discussion, "Integrating Written Language," National Council of Teachers of English Convention, New York City, Nov. 26, 1977.

27. Rees, Norma S. "Noncommunication Functions of Language in Children," *Journal of Speech and Hearing Disorders,* 1973, 38:98-110.

28. Werner, Heinz, and Bernard Kaplan. *Symbol Formation,* New York: Wiley, 1963.

29. Tough, Joan. *The Development of Meaning,* New York: Halstead Press, 1977.

30. There was no negative element in Leslie's utterance, but there was a steadily falling intonation pattern, which indicated a negative utterance for her at this stage of language development.

31. Robinson, W. P. *Language and Social Behavior,* Middlesex, England: Penguin Books, 1972.

32. Fleischman, Sid. "Laughter and Children's Literature," *The Horn Book Magazine,* October 1976.

33. *Op. cit.,* p. 104.

34. Brown, Roger. "Language and Categories," Appendix to J. S. Bruner, J. J. Goodnow, and G. A. Austin, *A Study of Thinking,* New York: Science Editions, 1962.

35. Vygotsky, L. S. *Thought and Language,* Cambridge, Mass.: MIT Press, 1962.

36. *Explorations in the Functions of Language* and *Learning How to Mean.*

37. *Explorations in the Functions of Language.*

38. *The Development of Meaning.*

39. *Ibid.,* pp. 80-81.

SUGGESTED READINGS

Britton, James. *Language and Learning,* Middlesex, England: Penguin Books, 1970.

Cazden, Courtney, Vera P. John-Steiner, and Dell Hymes (eds.). *Function of Language in the Classroom,* New York: Teachers College Press, Columbia University, 1972.

Halliday, Michael A. K. *Exploration in the Functions of Language,* London: Edward Arnold Publishers, 1973.

Rogers, Sinclair (ed.) *Children and Language: Readings in Early Language Socialization,* London: Oxford University Press, 1975.

Tough, Joan. *The Development of Meaning,* New York: Halstead Press, 1977.

2

Acquisition
of Conversational Skills

John (6:0): If you wonder what that noise is, that's me
   pounding.
Weeks: Is it?
Greg (2:5): That pounding, not me.
Weeks: Uh huh.
Greg: (unintelligible utterance)
John: What? You're probably anxious for Mom, aren't you,
   Greg?
About sixty seconds later:
John: Here's my little doggie laying down and here's my
   cookie. This is actually my ten thousand story apartment
   building.
Greg: /nami/, John. John, /nami/. You John. ("not me"
   probably).
Weeks: John what?
Greg: My talk John. (I was talking to John.)

   I was put in my place. Conversation has rules. Even an almost
two-and-a-half-year-old child can tell you that you are supposed to
answer only if you were spoken to. Conversation, in fact, has a myriad of

rules. It is amazing how many of them are observed by two-year-old children. And younger. But before we discuss the acquisition of conversational skills by young children, just what is a conversation?

A conversation is an interchange between at least two persons, a matter of alternate talking and listening. It is the unmarked register (style) of speech, the most neutral kind of English one can find. Language is used more for conversation than for any other purpose. With the exception of a hermit or a monk who has vowed silence, everyone can be expected to converse with someone during the course of an ordinary day. This includes very young children.

Before discussing how children learn to acquire conversational skills, it might be well to mention briefly some of the general characteristics of adult conversation. By definition, conversation must involve at least two individuals (a pair, a dyad, or partners). In reality, though perhaps not in theory, there is an upper limit to the number of persons who can participate in a conversation. By definition, also, turns are taken; otherwise it is a monologue (and this will be discussed later in the chapter). In addition, conversation ordinarily involves a largely verbal exchange in which speakers direct their gaze toward each other at least part of the time, depending on cultural norms.

In addition to these basic, generally definitional characteristics of adult conversation, Crystal and Davy[1] list three others: (1) The language of conversations is inexplicit. That is, participants rely on extra-linguistic context for their information, using substitute words such as *one, it,* and *that* rather than being specific. In addition to this, utterances are often incomplete. The listener can get the gist of the meaning from the context; so the remainder of the sentence would be redundant. (2) "Conversation is characterized by randomness of subject-matter, and a general lack of planning." The participants ordinarily do not know when the conversation starts how it will end (as opposed to such speech events as a debate or sermon). While participants *may* limit the topics or guide the course of the conversation, it is usually acceptable to change the subject. Along with changes of subject matter, participants may also alter the formality of the language, using different dialects or accents, as for telling jokes, etc. (3) What has been called "normal nonfluency": There are more "errors," slips of the tongue, hesitations, etc., than are *usually* found in speech events that are more planned in nature. Crystal and Davy[2] point out "the really significant fact about informal conversation is the toleration of these features when they occur, and indeed the expectation that they will occur. Perfect fluency in this variety tends to produce the wrong effect, for psychological and other reasons—one gets labelled a 'smooth' talker, for instance—which rather suggests that hesitation phenomena are of primary significance in determining the acceptability or non-acceptability of conversation."

Crystal and Davy's research concerned adult conversation. Children's conversations do not usually show this third characteristic until children are beyond the earliest language period. For example, child-language researchers have usually noted that conversations between parents and children in the two- and three-word utterance stage are not characterized by "normal nonfluency." Noam Chomsky's *Aspects of the Theory of Syntax*[3] included a child-language-acquisition model, and proposed that "primary linguistic data" available to children were "fairly degenerate in quality" and that much of the speech the child hears "consists of fragments and deviant expressions of a variety of sorts." Child-language researchers began to note that while "nonfluent" language is usual between adults in conversation, or at meetings, conferences, etc., when caretakers address young children, their speech consists of short, simple sentences, a great deal of repetition, and very few hesitancies and errors. A greatly simplified language model is offered to the child. It has also been noted that children's earliest language productions are "fluent" in that they usually do not consist of slips of the tongue, restarting of utterances, hesitancies, etc. A child's first utterances, such as "more milk," "Mommy dress," "Daddy go car," sound "fluent," though brief. However, we see that this is a passing phase, and soon children are indulging in the same kinds of normal nonfluency in conversational speech that adults do. See, for example, Jennie's monologue (age 5:0) at the end of this chapter.

Conversation as a Speech Event

Conversation is just one particular kind of speech event. Other examples are: a sermon, an inaugural address, a sales talk, or joke telling. There are certain essential components for any speech event, such as (1) a speaker; (2) at least one listener; (3) a code (a choice of language or dialect); (4) a form, or mode (speaking, sign language, writing, etc.); (5) a topic; and (6) a setting or situation.

When these components are combined in different ways, the resulting conversation may shift considerably. For example, when the speaker is a child and the listener is a strange man in a railroad station, the topic and formality of the language will differ from that of one child talking to another child in a sandbox. We will also see that children may ask their fathers for a favor in a very different way from the way they make similar requests to younger peers. By the time a child has acquired a vocabulary of fifty words, the child has also learned to use them very differently for different situations. Conversations are more carefully orchestrated than most participants ever realize. Children begin to acquire these in infancy, and studies reporting these activities are included in the next section.

Research on childhood conversations is in its infancy, and many aspects have scarcely been looked at. Other aspects, such as the asking and answering of questions, have been examined more thoroughly, but no aspect of the acquisition of conversational skills has been studied exhaustively. Any reader who has observed children carefully will be able to add to the body of information currently available. Research conducted before the 1970s was largely concerned with children's sentence structure, not with how children used their language. Current research, sometimes referred to as the study of discourse, communicative abilities, face-to-face interaction, or social interaction, as well as conversation, will be discussed in this chapter.

Prespeech "Conversations"

At what age do children begin to acquire conversational skills? What age must children be before parents consider them old enough to talk to? Hymes[4] reports that the Mohave and Tlingit Indians traditionally considered infants capable of understanding speech. Furthermore, the Tlingit believed that the talk of women was the source of conflict among men; so an amulet was placed in a baby girl's mouth to make her taciturn. The Ottawa believed that the cries of infants were meaningful and had specialists in their interpretation. In most Asian cultures, parents do not believe babies understand anything and tend to imitate the baby's sounds rather than talking to the babies. Hymes points out that the practice with infants and pets varies in our society, but as will be seen below, middle-class mothers frequently talk to their infants as though they could understand even though they do not believe they do.

M. A. K. Halliday, a British linguist, was among the first to point out that language is essentially the learning of a semantic system (rather than syntactic), and that the child is well on the way to having acquired a semantic system before he has any words at all. He "learns how to mean" long before he learns to express himself in words. Without any words at all, babies can let their mothers know they want to be picked up, want something to eat, want their mother to look at them, etc. By the 1970s a number of child-language researchers were beginning to study the prelanguage development of children because of the realization that language acquisition does not start with production of language but originates much earlier. Studies (as well as ordinary observation) indicate that conversation-like behavior begins at a very early age. Speech directed to prelinguistic infants is filled with affect rather than information, and serves to attract the infant's attention and establish a warm bond between the adult and the child, laying a foundation for language acquisition.

In a series of experiments conducted in Edinburgh, Scotland, and America, Colwyn Trevarthen and his colleagues looked at prespeech "conversations" between infants from birth to six years of age and their mothers. In a preliminary film study with Martin Richards and Jerome Bruner at Harvard, Trevarthen[5] looked for infant behavior that indicated that they perceived objects and people differently. In their weekly films (laboratory setting), they either suspended a small toy in front of the babies or filmed them with their mothers. They found "highly elaborate activity that was specific to communicating with persons" when the babies were with their mothers. Mothers were asked to "chat with her baby." None of the mothers considered this an odd request. Trevarthen states that the infants showed "two ways of spontaneously responding: one for the object and one for the mother. Most different were the expressions of face, voice and hands. We hypothesized two modes of psychological action: communication with persons, and 'doing' with objects."

Later experiments conducted by Trevarthen in Edinburgh with other colleagues corroborated the results at Harvard. Working with two-month-old babies, they found activity that they maintained could best be called "prespeech" activities because both the context in which it occurred and its form indicated that it was a rudimentary form of speaking by movements of lips and tongue. Sounds did not necessarily accompany the movements, though they might. Distinctive "hand-waving" movements that Trevarthen said were "developmentally related to the gestures or gesticulations of adults in 'eager' and 'graphic' conversation" accompany these prespeech activities. "We are now sure," Trevarthen states, "that, notwithstanding the importance of cultural development in the formation of language, both of speech and of gestures, the foundation for interpersonal communication between humans is 'there' at birth, and is remarkably useful by eight weeks when cognitive and memory processes are beginning."

Trevarthen goes on to claim that communication activity is much more complex than any other form of activity in infants at age two months. By the age of three weeks, their films show that infants approach persons and objects quite differently.

Just as conversation at any age requires a partner, this infant communication requires a partner. Looking at 97 three-month-old infants and their mothers in natural home settings, Freedle and Lewis[6] found that "when an infant vocalizes, the mother is most likely to respond with a vocalization of her own; her next most likely response is to either smile at, look at, or touch the infant. In like manner, given that the mother has just vocalized, the most likely behavior that the infant will engage in is also vocalization. To a much more reduced degree, infant vocalization is also likely to follow such maternally initiated behaviors as playing with, looking at, holding, or touching." Largely, then, vocalization begets vocalization.

On the basis of research spanning several years, Freedle and Lewis[7] propose four theories regarding the early development of conversational skills (restated):

1. Language behavior has its origins in a "general social communication system" (meaning system) to which words and grammar are added later.

2. The mother-infant interaction patterns, consisting of both vocalizations and movements, are designed to facilitate the growth of communication.

3. Of the elements of this primitive communication system, the vocalization behavior forms a subsystem that is more important than the nonvocal behaviors.

4. Prelanguage behaviors are situationally bound (for example, child behaves differently in mother's lap versus crib) even at very early ages. This forms a basis for the development of a complex semantic system such as develops later.

In summary, the foundation for communication between a child and others is present at birth—the child is born to talk. While great individual differences exist between children even at this point, other differences in the child's later language skills may be effected by the caretaker's (usually the mother) response to the child's communicative behavior—vocalizations in particular.

Early-Language Conversations

Turn taking is essential to conversation. Nothing can be comprehended if everyone talks at once, and if only one person talks, it is not conversation at all. This essential element is acquired early by children.

Children seem to learn *when* to talk, and something about *how* to talk before they know *what* to say. Brandon's early speech development offers an example.

By the time Brandon was 0:10, his repertoire consisted of eleven "words," one of which was /ɪzət/ (is it), a multipurpose word that he used principally for conversation. Five of his forms were used for designating animate objects: /di/ (Daisy) was the vestigial form used to refer to their dog Daisy, while /dayzət/ (perhaps Daisy + it) was the new name (he alternated between the two), /dʌ/ (duck), his name for his pet ducks, plus *mama* and *baby*, which he pronounced plainly and used appropriately. Two forms seemed to be used as descriptive terms: /ha/ (hot) was always used with pointing or touching to denote steam, a coffee cup, something that felt warm, etc., and /mmm/ which was used after tasting something that he enjoyed. *Uh uh* was said as he shook his head and sometimes pushed things away; it always meant "no." The ninth and tenth forms, /dæ/ (that) and /dɪ/ (this) were occasionally used with pointing in conversation, along with /ɪzət/ (is it). A ten- or fifteen-minute conversation with Brandon from 0:10 to 1:1 always included several /ɪzət/'s. It is a phrase his mother used repeatedly, with at least two different intonation patterns. She most often used the phrase as an acknowledgment of a statement, where a variant of "yes" might be used: "This is a good book." "Is it." Used in this way, it did not have a rising intonation, but fell, as an affirmation. Sometimes she used it as a question, with a rising intonation: "This is my duck." "Is it?" She also used the question, "What is it?" but less frequently.

A typical exchange between Brandon and myself was:

(Brandon was playing with a stuffed owl.)
Weeks: What ya doin' there?
Brandon: (No reply)
Weeks: Got a nice owl.
Brandon: /ɪzət/

Similar routines were repeated many times, and his /ɪzət/ response always sounded appropriate. He often pointed as he said /ɪzət/, but did not seem to expect a reply.

What I am suggesting is that /ɪzət/ was in a different category for Brandon than his other words. The other words referred to particular objects, or had specific meanings, while /ɪzət/ was something to say in order to maintain a conversation with an older person (a place holder). It certainly did not mean to him what "Is it" means to an adult. It was part of a routine. As part of a social routine, it has an element of meaning, just as greetings and other language formulas have social meaning apart from the words that are spoken. Gleason and Weintraub[8] have pointed out that in the case of routines, the child is not expected to learn the meaning of what he says—it is performance that counts. It is also the case that routines, by their very nature, are invariable whereas language in general, even when directed to young children, varies considerably. This sameness facilitates learning. If one tries to view language from Brandon's point of view, "Is it" might seem like a routine because it was a consistent way for his mother to respond in conversation. Brandon heard it interspersed in conversation in just the way he used it, that is, with the same intonation, and after someone had just finished directing some speech to the conversational partner.

Some of the things Brandon did not do include: (1) interrupt the flow of conversation with /ɪzət/, (2) reply to speech directed to another person, or (3) necessarily appear to expect a reply after /ɪzət/; that is, it was possible to end the conversation at this point, except when /ɪzət/ was used with a rising intonation (not the usual case).

At this age (0:10 to 1:1) Brandon did not expect to be included in adult conversation in the room. He paid attention and responded only when an adult was looking directly at him and talking.

Of the children mentioned in the Introduction who are more than 2:0, John was the only one who included himself in adult conversations from 2:0 to 3:0. He often placed himself within the conversation group of adults rather than playing with toys or entertaining himself in some other way. During this time, particularly from about 2:3 to 2:6, as he sat among adults who were conversing, he would often insert "a door" into the conversation. He appeared to be paying attention to the speaker, and to be listening. These were conversations which were not directed to him, but were between adults. He never said it except during a pause, and he appeared to consider it an appropriate thing to say. His timing—the *when*—was impeccable. At this age, he had a good vocabulary and was producing some two- and three-word utterances, and in direct conversation with him, what he said was usually meaningful. In the case of adult conversations, one could guess that he understood little of what was said, and perhaps "a door" seemed as sensible to him as anything else he heard. It was a word he had acquired at about 2:1, and perhaps he just enjoyed hearing the sound of it. (There is always the remote possibility that I am spelling it wrong, and that he was saying "Adore!") The *how* was correct, too, in that he used appropriate pitch, volume, and intonation.

Jennie used a mid-vowel (*a*) as a multipurpose word to use in conversation when she had no other response to make. She carried on conversations lasting up to fifteen minutes with no reply except a variation of this vowel, which could range from a bright, happy *ah* to a whiny *uh*. As was the case with Brandon's "is it," Jennie's *ah* seemed to function as a conversational place holder but had no other meaning. She used her multipurpose vowel innumerable times between 1:3 and 2:3 in such exchanges as the following:

Weeks: Go tell the boys dinner is ready.
Jennie (raced to the room where they were playing and shouted): Ah!
(John and Greg knew if Jennie was giving them an order in a loud voice they should investigate, and they came to see what I wanted.)

Greg: I'm hungry.
Jennie (nodding her head vigorously): Ah (She was hungry too.)

Weeks: Would you like to tell me about this book? You like this one, don't you?
Jennie: Ah
Weeks: What's that?
Jennie: Ah
Weeks: Would you like to turn the page of the book?
Jennie: Ah

Weeks: Why don't you talk to Mommy on the telephone?
Jennie (picking up toy phone): Ah ah ah ah

Jennie was slow in producing language, but she knew when someone talked to her that it was appropriate to answer, and she replied even though she had to improvise for answers.

In participating in conversations, then, it was found that children demonstrate a knowledge of *when* to say something, even if they have nothing to say. In the examples offered here, it was the case that children were actively engaging themselves in conversation with adults—they were participants in a speech event. It was not a case of their having something to communicate and desperately wanting to tell someone about it. In such cases, children typically interrupt the flow of conversation, talking at inappropriate times, trying to get the attention of either the speaker or the listener. It takes time for a child to learn to control his output—to learn not to say what he has to say until others have stopped talking. Individuals of any age experience this contrast. What is examined here, then, is the slower-paced kind of conversation in which a person can demonstrate what he knows about the skills of conversation because he's not overly eager to say something. I have been looking here more at form than at substance.

The Mechanics of Conversation

Conversation does not just happen. As was mentioned above, it is very carefully orchestrated, and some of that orchestration will be discussed in this section. *How* language is used by the child may indicate whether or not the listener is younger or older than the speaker, how well the speaker knows the listener, whether or not the speaker considers the listener superior in some way, and whether or not the speaker considers the listener a member of a peer group. Some of these aspects of how children become competent conversationalists have been examined, while some have not. Some of the essentials of conversation to be discussed in this section are: greetings and farewells, gaining the attention of a prospective listener and initiating a conversation, making requests and issuing directives, requesting clarification when something was not entirely clear, interrupting the speaker (or learning *not* to interrupt the speaker), learning to remain silent, choosing a conversational partner, and choosing appropriate topics for conversation.

Greetings and Farewells   Greetings and farewells generally have been referred to in the literature of child language acquisition as *routines.* Ferguson[9] has also called greetings and farewells *politeness formulas,* and says that they are universal in human speech communities. Universal aspects of language may be expected to appear in child language before nonuniversals, and indeed, we find that greetings and farewells are among the earliest bits of language behavior acquired by children.

This universality of greetings, in particular, is interesting here because one of the greetings to be discussed was not taught—was not a "prefabricated routine," to use Roger Brown's label. Does the greeting fulfill such a primitive need that greeting routines will be invented, if not taught?

In this regard, Brandon's "greetings" may be relevant. When he was just 1:0, I spent most of a day with him. (Previous to this I had spent only short periods of time with him, and he didn't seem to remember me.) When I arrived, I said, "Hi, Brandon." He gave me a pleasant look, but didn't actually smile. In an effort to make friends, I kneeled down in front of him (he may have considered this a physical feat!), and chatted for another minute or two. As the day went on he seemed to enjoy having me do things for him, and I felt that we had become friends. Two weeks later, I spent six days with him. On the first of these days, I greeted him with "Hi, Brandon" and he smiled, obviously remembering me. Then he put his hands up over his head with his fingers just touching each other on top of his head. I said, "Oh, what a good trick!" giving him the kind of lavish praise for a small accomplishment that middle-class Americans often do with small children. He went on to perform all the physical feats he could think of: he leaned back as far as he could, he put his hands on the floor in front of him and looked out between his legs, and then he stood up and cocked his head to one side and smiled. Each day after that when I arrived, I greeted him in the same way ("Hi, Brandon!") and each day he responded by performing one, two, or three physical feats for me.

Two weeks later (he was now 1:1), I spent part of a day with him. Whereas when I was arriving each morning, he was prepared with one or two tricks to do for me, this time he was surprised to see me. After I greeted him, he smiled and then averted his eyes and I could tell he was trying to think of a trick to do for me. Within a second or so he looked at me and smiled again, and got down on his hands and knees and crawled a short distance. By this age he was walking easily and crawling was a novelty—a physical feat of sorts.

This was what evolved as Brandon's way of responding to my greeting. It was not the way he greeted everyone. For example, when his mother came to pick him up after work, she greeted him, and he consistently pointed to something in the room, or touched something and said /dæ/ (that). She responded by commenting on the object he pointed to. He pointed to something different each day, as though he wanted her to be acquainted with all the things he saw regularly, but which she didn't see. He was not responding to her in the same way she greeted him.

His way of greeting his father when he came home from work was different yet. He handed him a book and expected his father to read it to him immediately, or a toy and expected him to play with it briefly. His father always obliged. One day his mother got him a new hand puppet, a large one that covered his whole arm once he had it on properly. He was very pleased with it, and apparently decided to show it to his father when he arrived home. Brandon heard his father at the door and started running down the hall to greet him, but the puppet almost came off his arm. He continued running down the hall, struggling with the puppet, but wouldn't even look at his father until he could get the puppet positioned on his arm so he could show it to him. By this time, his father was waiting for him, but Brandon averted his gaze until he had the puppet ready, then he smiled and held out his arm with the puppet so his father could see it. The toy was not an accessory to the greeting, but rather it seemed to play a primary role. If Brandon didn't have a new toy or book to show his father, he showed him an old one. He always had something to hand his father as he greeted him.

His greeting to each of three individuals (his mother, father, and me) was consistent, and the greeting for each person was individualized. I was a non-family member who didn't know him so well; so he showed me what he could do. His parents knew what he could do, so he didn't do that for them. For his mother, he showed things he associated with each day while she was gone (never one of his own toys or things he brought from home). For his father, who often read to him and played with him, he showed toys and expected to be entertained briefly. It can be seen from this that the usual definition of *routine* does not apply. There was nothing conventionalized or "prefabricated" about these routines. Neither were they echoes of what had been said to him (these are certain to come later). They were not even verbal. They were greeting routines that he fabricated himself. Brandon had apparently discerned that some greeting behavior was appropriate to the situation, but didn't know what to say or how to say it. How could he guess that all he needed to do was to repeat what was said to him, minus his name? His greeting behavior was unique except for the *when*. The timing, in fact, was all that made it clear that it was a greeting.

On the other hand, I have noticed repeatedly that while children have learned to greet a person when they enter the room, for example, it takes some children several years to learn that you don't greet a person *every* time they enter the room. Adults, for example, usually greet each other upon the first encounter of the day, and thereafter during that day, even though a period of several hours elapses between conversations, talk may resume without greeting. This is true even for family members. A kiss, a greeting of some kind, a question regarding the health and welfare of the family member, is in order upon arising in the morning, but not later in the day, unless one member has left and returned again. I have noticed, however, that children, sometimes up to ages six or eight, will often say "Hi!" to me each time I reenter the room in which they are playing. Perhaps it is more often a bid for attention than a way to start a conversation, however.

Greeting Variation According to Age of Addressee: There are many ways in which children are usually required to use forms of respect to older persons. Parents remind children to say *please*, or they are told to address adults by title (Mr. or Mrs. plus surname) even though the adults call each other by their first names. Age differentiation in greetings appears at an early age. By 2:11 John seemed to have a clear notion about who was younger or older than himself, and would say "Hi" to younger children (or initiate a conversation with them without a greeting) but would wait for an older child to greet him or start a conversation. Fred, who was somewhat more gregarious than John, made it a habit (about 4:9) to introduce himself to new neighbors, older children who walked past his home, or people he saw other places. However, when he wanted to talk to children younger than himself, he simply started a conversation without an introduction or greeting. When he was 4:0, I took him to a park where there was a large sand box about 30 feet in diameter and we stayed for more than an hour. During this time other children came and went. If Fred decided to play with younger children, he simply went over to them and started a conversation. But when a boy about eight or nine years old came and settled down across the sand box from Fred, Fred started to walk toward him and said, "Hi. My name's Fred. How are you?" The boy looked up at him and stared. Finally he said, "Hi," and Fred sat down and they played together for 15 or 20 minutes.

Simplification versus Elaboration: Ferguson[10] discusses politeness formulas as having norms which can be either simplified or elaborated upon. He notes that in American English during the past forty years the greeting "How are you" has been simplified first to "Hiya!" and then to "Hi!" This short form has become a very common one, and is one often preferred by children. At age 4:0, Fred greeted everyone with a simple "Hi!" except his preschool teacher, whom he greeted with "Good morning!"

In order to determine what Fred's attitudes were about greetings, I asked him (4:9) to make some telephone calls on a toy telephone. He called his doctor, a neighbor, and some friends. He greeted them all with "Hi!" I asked him if he ever said "hello" to anyone, and he studied my face to see if I was serious. "I never say 'hello' " he answered, and it was clear he thought it was a peculiar question. The simplified *hi* had become standard form (except for greeting his teacher).

One expects children to use longer, more elaborated forms only for special occasions of some kind, if at all. Jennie, however, used elaborated forms of farewells regularly, often inappropriately. For example, at 3:6 she started saying "Good-bye and good luck!" to her father when he left for work in the morning. At 5:0, as she and her parents were leaving on a trip, I said, "Have a good trip!" and within a few seconds she said to me, "Good-bye, and have a good trip!" Gregory corrected her, "No! We're the ones who are taking a trip!"

Two other children, Ryan and Ricky (3:11 and 7:10), who stayed overnight at our home recently, said "Have a nice day at work!" rather than "Good-bye!" as my husband left the house in the morning.

It took forty years for the greeting "How are you?" to be reduced to "Hi!" and now we see routines being elaborated again. In some cases, routines are used at times when nothing was used before, such as (at least with young waiters and waitresses) when being seated in a restaurant ("Have a nice dinner!") or upon being served ("Enjoy your dinner!"). Jennie's elaborated forms are not idiosyncratic; she has picked up something that has become common with young adults.

Initiation of Conversation   Schegloff[11] points out that a greeting serves as a summons for the right to talk.[12] When the second speaker responds to the greeting, he is granting the right to talk to the first speaker. Then the conversation proceeds. For children this summons often consists of the name of the person being addressed: "Mommy!" and it will be repeated until the mother gives her attention to the child. Scollon[13] reports that Brenda (2:0) used "Hi" in this way. She expected more than a simple response; she expected to be able to start a conversation:

> Brenda: Hi!
> Scollon: Hi. How're you doing? (Then, continuing his conversation with another person) Let's see, piece of paper. Tri-X.
> Brenda: Hi!
> Scollon (to Brenda): Hi. Hi. How are you? Been a long time since you saw this set up, isn't it?

It may be seen from this that a greeting may be just a greeting, or it may serve to initiate a conversation. Scollon reports that during the hour following the above exchange, Brenda used *hi* seven times with him. In most cases he answered as if it were a greeting, but Brenda considered it as a summons and continued trying to talk to him.

Brenda also used *here,* accompanied by handing the listener something, as a summons. Scollon maintains that Brenda did not need a summons for her mother, and perhaps not for her older sister Charlotte. He offers the following rules for establishing the right to talk:[14]

(1) When the right to talk has not been established, Brenda uses *hi, here,* or the combination of handing plus topic to initiate interactions with Suzanne and me. [Suzanne is Scollon's wife.]

(2) With the mother the right to talk is permanently established.

(3) With Charlotte the right to talk may or may not be permanently established since *here* was only used a few times and when it was, it failed.

(4) When the right to talk temporarily lapses, but Brenda is still audience to the interaction, she regains the floor by repeating her utterance.

(5) When the right to talk temporarily lapses and Brenda is excluded as participant, she becomes unintelligible until the right to talk is reestablished.

Leslie repeatedly used "Know what?" as a summons for the right to talk. Garvey and Hogan[15] studied middle-class children, 3:6 to 5, in natural play situations and noted that "Know what?" was a most frequent opener for conversation. It is a question that requires a negative answer. Adults use a similar conversational opener: "Did you hear about _____ ?" The listener is not expected to answer in the affirmative and then give all the details. The question implies that the speaker is offering information on the topic suggested.

As this conversational opener may suggest, the most common way to start a conversation is to ask a question, rhetorical or otherwise. Mishler[16] has looked at conversations that start with questions. The children in his experiment were first-graders and the adults were both teachers and other adults in the classroom. He found that when adults initiate the conversation by asking a question, they retain control over its course by successive questioning. However, when children ask an adult a question, the adult regains control by responding with a question. Children use both methods in conversing with each other.

It should be reiterated here that this is a classroom behavior. Teachers ask questions so children will be forced to think, search for answers, etc., as opposed to having things made too easy by the teacher giving them answers. Adults in the home situation usually do not view themselves in this role, and do not necessarily try to control the conversation by asking more questions than they answer.

Ervin-Tripp and Miller[17] have pointed out that answering questions is one of the first clearly discourse-bound obligations to which children are sensitive. In fact, their responsiveness to questions is so strong that adults often frame questions simply to occupy a turn or keep conversation going, when nobody cares about the information offered or received. It should be mentioned here, however, that there are cultural differences in the necessity to answer questions. The Yakima Indian children I worked with did not answer questions as frequently as non-Indian children did, nor do Yakima adults feel obligated to answer questions at the time the question is asked. A thoughtful answer is considered preferable to a fast answer; so questions are sometimes answered the next day, or on the next visit. Judging from the middle-class families I have observed, it seems to be the case that these children are actively taught an obligation to answer questions. Parents are heard to reprimand children, "You were asked a question!" if children do not answer voluntarily and immediately.

Adults sometimes try to open conversations with children with a compliment instead of a question. One might think that a compliment would be easy to respond to. One could simply say "Thank you," or perhaps just smile. But compliments are often difficult, for adults as well as children, to accept graciously. By 2:6 Fred seemed to be particularly embarrassed by flattering comments by strangers, or by a stranger trying to start a conversation with him in a solicitous way. He was at a complete loss for words, and his usual response was to hit some member of his family. If a stranger talked to him in a matter-of-fact way or just asked simple questions, Fred answered just as matter-of-factly, but he seemed to have no appropriate response for flattery or for a solicitous manner. Goffman[18] says "embarrassment has to do with unfulfilled expectations." Children's expectations may not always be what adults think they are, and so adults may not recognize children's reaction to embarrassment for what it is. Children need to learn how to show their embarrassment in appropriate ways, or to try to conceal it.

What kinds of speech acts do children use that do *not* serve well to initiate conversation? Ervin-Tripp[19] wondered how old children are when they stop commenting on passing objects ("Big truck." "Bird."). This is undoubtedly an individual matter, but I realized after pondering the question that I still comment on passing objects when I am traveling. "There's another Highway Patrolman." "The hills are nice and green." I do not expect a reply, and I do not get one. I have no expectation that these remarks will start a conversation. Neither are such observations at a party or large gathering conversation starters: "Big crowd tonight." "Nice paintings." The best a polite listener can do with such remarks is agree, and the conversation is back where it started. However, children often expect, and wait for, this agreement. At about 2:0, for example, Leslie would say, upon hearing an airplane, "pwane," and wait for agreement, "Yes, there's an airplane." She would repeat the observation several times if the listener did not acknowledge it the first time. Even this, of course, qualified as conversation. It is a verbal interchange between two individuals. Adults are often concerned about introducing topics that will help a conversation continue. Children are not concerned about this at early ages. Perhaps it is our expectations about what these comments will accomplish that changes more than the simple fact of making them.

Garvey[20] examined the ability of 36 preschool children (3:6 to 5:7) to issue and respond to requests from peers. The children were observed in a well-furnished laboratory playroom. Garvey found that even the youngest subjects were able to formulate both direct ("Gimme that ladder.") and indirect ("Father, can you take the baby?") requests, and respond appropriately to them. Although requests usually require some action as an appropriate response, Garvey found that most requests were answered verbally as well. Many requests, such as "Let's play mothers and fathers," initiated conversation as a result of the request being granted. However, to the extent that requests are often responded to principally with action, they are not as reliable as questions for initiating conversation.

Mueller,[21] observing children from 3:6 to 5:6 in spontaneous verbal interaction in an unstructured situation, concluded that when a child's utterance is a command or a question, it has the best chance of being responded to by another child listener. When children failed to get a response, it was often because they did not have the attention of the listener at the time they spoke—they did not use a summons or had not gained eye contact before speaking. Mueller had expected that he would find dramatic improvements in communication success between ages 3:6 to 5:6, but he failed to. The reason was that even the youngest children (3:6) were successful in receiving replies to their messages. Communicative skills are developed earlier than this.

As I have already pointed out, certain aspects of communicative skills are being developed in the first few months of life, at least with the infants observed by Trevarthen, and Freedle and Lewis, as mentioned earlier. One of the reasons many child-language researchers have expected abilities to develop late is that Piaget[22] has said children do not learn to converse before about age five. He observed twenty children, ages four to seven, in the Maison des Petits in Geneva, and of those who were in what he called Stage I, none were engaging in conversation at all. Even when they seemed to be addressing someone in particular, they were, he maintained, talking to themselves. They seemed not to be seeking answers to questions or to be attending in any meaningful way to what the other children said. How can the findings of such a careful observer as Piaget be accounted for, in view of more recent findings to the contrary? Piaget offers the most likely explanations himself. First, he suggests that children need to be observed in settings other than the nursery school, such as "at play in public gardens, etc." The Maison des Petits may have been unique. The teachers in the school pointed out that up until the age of about five, the children almost always work alone. This does not coincide with what observers usually report in this decade, and in this country. Second, Piaget found, from the work of other researchers, that children with different scholastic environments in other countries, such as Germany, followed other patterns. Third, he points out that children talking among themselves or with their parents behave differently. Language in the school and in the home may be expected to be different. If we look only at language in one setting (the school) between children of similar ages, while a limited variety of activities are being engaged in, we will find a limited range of language registers (styles) in use. Perhaps the range of language varieties available to the children in the Maison des Petits were limited. We will never know. In my research I have observed children in a wide variety of settings, such as in their home, my home, restaurants, airports, at nursery school, and at bathtime, and have observed that the language used varies greatly with the setting, the person being addressed, and the child's interpretation of the kind of language suitable for the occasion.

Another reason for low expectations of children's discourse was the popularity of studies of referential communication such as that of Glucksberg, Krauss, and Weisberg.[23] In experiments such as this, children were given language tasks that were very narrowly defined, such as being asked to describe a novel form in such a way that another child who has not seen the form will be able to identify it. Such a task turns out to be different and more difficult for a child than communicating about activities that the child devises. A much larger proportion of recent research has stressed naturalistic environments for observations and experiments designed to discover what language capabilities children have.

In summary, then, conversations are initiated by children and attended to by other children at earlier ages than has been thought in the past. Greetings may serve merely as a greeting (as when individuals pass each other on the street or on the playground) or they may serve as a summons for the right to talk—to initiate a conversation. Other such initiators are "Know what?" or other questions that are less routine in nature. Compliments and remarks about passing objects are unreliable conversation initiators. Requests and directives may initiate a conversation, but since this is not their usual purpose, and since they may often serve to change the subject, they will be discussed separately.

Requests and Directives   Directives comprise a large proportion of children's utterances, perhaps as much as 50 percent, and are therefore an important aspect to be studied. Ervin-Tripp has written extensively on requests and directives (orders), regarding both adults and children, and this section draws heavily on her research.[24] She has pointed out that directives may take a wide variety of syntactic forms, occurring "systematically, according to familiarity, rank, territorial location, difficulty of task, whether or not a duty is normally expected, and whether or not non-compliance is likely." Adult directives may take the form of an imperative: "Take off your shoes" or "Put your blocks away" but more often take some other form. They may appear to be statements, "Your shoes are muddy" or "You didn't eat all of your vegetables." Also, the imperative may be embedded in a question, "Would you like to *put your blocks away*?" (where the italic portion is the imperative) or "Can I ask you to *take your feet off my head*?" Statements of need are often intended as directives. "I'm hungry" or "I need help putting these toys away." Hints are more subtle directives, and typically require interpretation on the part of the listener: "The cookies are all gone" (= "Give me some more cookies.") or "Would you bring me my sweater?" (= "Please close the window.").

There is a difference in formality that may be recognized in these varying styles of directives. In addition to an informal system, Ervin-Tripp suggests that there are at least two systems of deference, or politeness, which are available. The first she calls a "system of honorifics which embroider a selected form. These include repetitions, naming, *OK*, *please*, and embeddings. An extreme case would be 'Daddy, would you give me some cookies, OK, Daddy, please?' " The other is a system by which the person addressed is given the verbal guise of a choice: "Is there any more ice cream?" or "Is Mr. Smith in?" When such questions are asked in the usual social context, they are not at all ambiguous.

The question arises, then, regarding how many of these styles of directives children use and in what situation, how many of them they recognize as directives (that is, how many they act upon), and what social information they are able to infer from hearing them used by other individuals.

Production of Directives: Looking first at the question of the age at which various forms are produced, children's first directives are usually in the form of imperatives, for example, "more," or "up," and are often accompanied by gestures. Ervin-Tripp suggests that embedded requests begin to appear by about 2:6 but that the directive always includes the thing wanted, for example, "Where's my doll?" However, she notes that in some cases, these questions, which appear to be directives, are also accompanied by searching by the child and so may be considered egocentric speech rather than a directive.

However, by this age, Jennie was using hints that were syntactically ambiguous, though gestures specified the thing wanted. If not precisely hints (in that interpretation was clear), they at least represented an indirect approach. At 2:7, for example, Jennie saw that Greg and John each had a cookie, and she wanted one, too. She pointed to their cookies and said, "John have. Greg have." She got the cookie. Hints for tastes of food being eaten by other family members were routine by 2:9. At this age, she saw her father eating a bacon and avocado sandwich (she had already eaten), and asked, "Dat for?" pointing to the sandwich. Knowing she had eaten, he ignored her question. She continued to stand near, and said, "Mmmm. 'Cado good." Her father finally gave her a bite, and she left.

Garvey[25] found that children 3:6 to 3:10 did not hint, when conversing with each other. Jennie's hinting, it should be noted, was always directed at persons older than herself, though not necessarily adults. As Ervin-Tripp suggests, hints are probably used by young children more regarding food, or state of hunger, than for any other purpose. A large proportion of hints at all ages (up to thirteen) in my data are about food, and reflect a reluctance to ask (someone other than the principal caretaker) directly for what is wanted. For example, I asked Ricky (7:10), if he would like to have waffles and bacon for breakfast. No response. Would he like bacon and eggs? No response. How about cereal and toast? "Did you say pancakes?" he asked. He was giving me a choice, making it easy for me to say, "No, I didn't say that," and also lessening the chance of embarrassment for himself. He was noticeably relieved and happy when I replied, "Why, sure you can have pancakes. I don't know why I didn't say pancakes!"

In data reviewed by Ervin-Tripp, an Italian child used the past-tense form "I wanted to have some raisins" as a request at 2:8. Embedded directives are not unusual at this age: "Would you push this?" and "Would you stand up on my roller skate?" at 2:9. "Why aren't you drinking your coffee?" (Italian), 3:2, "Are you going to leave the toy here?" (Turkish), 3:5, and "You could give one to me," 3:8, are other examples of directives. Embedding becomes more frequent as children get older.

Fred and Leslie's mother used the inclusive *we* in addressing them, and Fred (but not Leslie) frequently used this form about 2:4 to 3:0. For example, at 2:6, he had just gotten into a bathtub of water that was too hot for him, and he asked "Are we too warm?"

Dore[26] found tag questions used by children from 2:10 to 3:6 to add deference, or politeness, to directives. Such directives as "You take these, okay?" (in which okay is the tag question) is equivalent to "Take these!" plus "Is that all right with you?" Dore points out that utterances of the form "That's a zebra, right?" were often addressed to adults even when the child seemed to be sure of the identification of the object.

Ervin-Tripp[27] gives some nice examples of "elaborate oblique strategems." "Six-year-old in supermarket: 'Can I have a penny?' Mother (surprised at small request): 'Why yes.' Ten minutes later, at another stop, child deposits penny in gum machine." In order to understand the child's strategy here, one must know that the child would have been denied the penny if she had asked for it when they reached the gum machine. It was also necessary for the child to anticipate the second stop at the time they were making the first one.

Garvey[28] offers another example, this time between two four-year-olds at nursery school:

A approaches a large toy car that B has just been sitting on:
A Pretend this was my car.
B No!
A Pretend this was our car.
B All right.
A Can I drive your car?
B Yes, okay. (Smiles and moves away from car)
A (Turns wheel and makes driving noises)

We see here that the hypothetical joint possession of the car was what turned the trick. Garvey comments "Skill in the use of verbal strategies by the time that speech is fluent but not mature implies a degree of competence in the pragmatic aspect of language which is as yet poorly understood."

Ervin-Tripp[29] lists permission directives ("May I have a match?") as a form that was found in adult speech, but they were too rare in children's speech to study. She suggests that they are possibly addressed upward more often than downward in rank. I also found this to be the case. At 2:6 Fred had food on his face and wanted it cleaned off. He asked, "Shall we wipe a face?" About this same time I took Fred to a restaurant where he had eaten before and he remembered that they gave scribble paper and pencils to children. He asked the waitress, "Shall we have a pencil?" She did not understand this as a directive but brought a pencil as soon as I explained what Fred meant. More often, however, the "shall we" form was associated with food: "Shall we have a cookie?"

There is little data for establishing age ranges and orders of acquisition of the various forms of directives. First forms are simple imperatives and gestures. By the time children are five or six, they are using fairly complex strategies. It may be assumed that beyond the first forms, a wide range of individual and cultural differences will be found. In some cultures devious means, such as hints, are not favored. Even in this country, there is a wide range of attitudes and practice regarding the use of indirect forms of directives. For example, the mother may encourage them as being more polite while the father discourages them as being devious—a little less than honest. It can also be seen that the amount of exposure a child has to indirect requests will have a bearing on how early he learns to produce them and interpret them.

Interpretation of Directives: Failure to comply to a directive does not necessarily indicate a lack of comprehension because there may be numerous reasons why a child does not wish to comply, even though he understands. Therefore, *interpretation* refers here to the child's appropriate response. All other things being equal, it may be assumed that a child will interpret an imperative without any difficulty. Embedded imperatives ("Would you please *finish your breakfast?*") are usually just as easy to interpret. Need statements and permission directives seem to be readily interpreted by children also. Ervin-Tripp[30] points out that "the belief that imbedded directives might be hard to understand rests on the assumption that young children go through a literal interpretation of syntax, rather than employ easier interpretative strategies requiring less verbal processing." Children need only to have had some experience with such forms to be able to interpret them correctly.

Ervin-Tripp reports that a Turkish child at two did not interpret "Do you know any stories?" as a directive. It was necessary to use the imperative, "Tell us one." In other situations, however, we find that while question directives and hints are less explicit than imperatives, some children are interpreting them correctly between the ages of two and three. For example, when Jennie was 2:6, I walked into her room and found her coat on the floor. I asked, "What's your coat doing on the floor?" Jennie picked up the coat, went to her closet, held the coat up and said, "Can't reach!" She was, indeed, too short to reach the hook where it belonged. She had correctly interpreted the question to mean "Hang it up!" and she explained why she couldn't. (The same question directed to Fred, age thirteen, would have gotten a response such as "Amassing an assortment of wrinkles!" I have found no preschoolers, however, who make a joke out of such directives by treating them literally.)

Dore[31] reports two exchanges between nursery-school children, aged 2:10 and 3:3, and their teacher, in which the children's replies sound somewhat inappropriate unless one analyzes the questions in the way the children did, as a directive and not a request for information:

> Teacher: John, are you finished? (= Put the block away!)
> John: They're out 'cause I'm sorting them.

John's reply explains (appropriately) *why* he has not put the blocks away, rather than replying directly to the question as to whether or not he has finished with them.

> Teacher: Did you make a hole for the grapefruit seed?
>   (= Make a hole!)
> Child: I wan' take one of those.

In this case, the child ignores what appears to be a question for information, and explains that he or she wants to get a seed out before making the hole in the soil. It is obvious in both of these examples that the child is making the correct interpretation of the teacher's intentions rather than responding to the sentence structure. That is, the child is *not* responding in a simple way to what sounds like a question for information.

Shatz[32] studied 11 female and 7 male middle-class children, aged 1:7 to 2:10. In a play situation, the children heard directives of the type: "Can you fit the ball in the truck?" and "Why don't you put the dog in the car?" She found that direct imperatives were no more likely to elicit action from the children than were more indirect requests. The more sophisticated the child is in terms of his language-production capabilities, the more likely he is to respond with language as well as action. Shatz suggests that children come to a communicative situation strongly biased to respond to language with action—that action is the *basic* mode of response at this age. She points out that in situations where the language directed to the child and the context work together to preclude an action interpretation, and the situation suggests a verbal response, children from 1:7 to 2:4 have the ability to respond verbally. The action responses, therefore, do not result from the child's inability to respond otherwise. Jennie's picking her coat up to show me she couldn't reach (supplemented by language) is the usual way for a child of this age to respond. But more importantly, children assume that when an adult speaks to them, it is to tell them to do something! They try to figure out what it is the adult expects and act accordingly.

Ervin-Tripp suggests that when an experiment alternates feasible and nonfeasible acts in such embedded imperatives as "Why don't you . . . ?" the proportion of action responses is much higher for feasible acts than in the context "Can you . . . ?" with alternating feasible and nonfeasible acts. She suggests that around age three, children learn to respond to "Why don't you . . . ?" with a "because . . ." response, particularly if one is asking the child to perform an unfeasible act.

The ability of children to respond appropriately to hints and question directives depends upon the child's social sophistication more than on his linguistic abilities.

Social Variation in Directives: As soon as children are old enough to make requests of any kind, they differentiate the directives they produce according to a variety of factors. The first differentiation is between those persons the children will make a request of and those to whom they will not. For example, they will ask mother for a glass of milk, but not a stranger. This difference between treatment of familiar and unfamiliar persons begins in infancy and lasts a lifetime and is reflected in language throughout a person's life. This is sometimes referred to as a formal/informal contrast and the general (greatly oversimplified) rule is that the most informal language is used with the most familiar persons, and the most formal language with the least familiar persons. Who are unfamiliar persons to a small child? Sometimes it may be the case that the child judges the father to be enough less familiar than the mother to warrant different treatment. Ervin-Tripp[33] offers an example of such differentiation (but, of course, we don't know *why* the child differentiates). In this case, the child's empty milk glass was set at her place at the table, next to a bottle of milk. Her milk was usually poured before she was put up to the table. The child said to her mother, "Mommy, I want milk." Under the same circumstances, she said to her father, "What's that? Milk. My milk, Daddy. Yes, it's your milk. Daddy, yours. Yours Daddy? OK, yours. OK, it's mine. It's milk, Daddy. Yes, it is. You want milk, Daddy? I have some, thank you. Milk in there, Daddy? Yes. Daddy, I want some, please? Please, Daddy, huh?" This would seem to be a good example of the system of honorifics which embroider a form. In contrast, the request directed to her mother was as straightforward as it could be. We have no information here as to the number of hours per week the child spends with one parent as compared with the other.

By the time children are two to three years old, they begin addressing persons of different ages differently. Ervin-Tripp cites a study by Lawson[34] in which he recorded the directives of a two-year-old child, who had essentially three syntactic forms to be used as requests. In a sample of 50 directives at nursery school and 50 at home, it was found that she gave almost entirely simple imperatives to her peers, but to adults she used either desire statements (56 percent), or questions (38 percent) including permission requests.

MacWhinney[35] found similar variation in request forms produced by Hungarian children. The children used "gimme" to other children. Politeness formulas, such as *thank you*, were used at first only when an adult told them to. By 1:8, a child used a form similar to *please* when making a request of the mother. To other adults he used a polite request form in Hungarian by 1:6. By 2:2 this child also used the polite form to another child when he wanted something. Children learn the persuasive powers of polite forms very early.

We see from this sampling of data from recent literature that children employ (and comprehend) a wide variety of styles in issuing directives. Age and familiarity of addressee are the two more important variables, but the kind of task, and the probability of compliance (wheedling or polite forms may be viewed as necessary) are also factors. Directives tend to become less direct and more devious as children grow older, though there is a wide range of individual differences in this respect.

Requests for Clarification   Because conversation is a matter of communicating, it is essential for partners to understand each other. When one person does not understand what the other has said, it is usual to ask the speaker to repeat what was said. Or listeners may repeat what they thought they heard, and expect the speaker to verify it. A request for clarification follows: (Garvey,[36] children are 4:0, and are playing house)

Y	X
1. Father, can I come?	2. What?
3. *Can I come?*	4. *What?*
5. *Can I come?*	6. *Call?*
7. *Come.*	8. *Yes.*
9. I have to watch the baby.	

The italicized utterances include the request for clarification ("What?") and then the request for verification, or confirmation ("Call?") and the response that clarifies the misunderstanding ("Come."). If the italicized text is deleted, the remainder of the conversation remains intact. The request for clarification and the response are a digression from the speech act in progress—subordinate to the rest of the conversation.

Sometimes the speaker adds more information or rephrases what was said when the listener does not understand the first time:

> Leslie (3:7): Look at the light. I wish I get that light down. Where it's turn . . . where its get off?
> Weeks: *Hmmm?*
> Leslie: *Where's its get off? That light off?*
> Weeks: Oh, there's a switch by the door.

It is somewhat surprising to see how often children repeat what they have said, or expand upon it when a simple *yes* would seem to suffice. For example:

> Fred (3:9) (He is building with blocks): And then we'll put this on top. This will be where to get a drink a water. This will be all in the shaped-order.
> Weeks: A shape-order?
> Fred: Yes, a shape-order—an order shaped like a stack.

In addition to the expanded statement, Fred's response to my question was more clearly articulated than his original statement had been. There was more of a pause between syllables and words, and consonants, in particular, were clearly enunciated. Bloom, Miller, and Hood[37] offer a similar example:

(Bloom is reading a magazine to Gia)
Gia (2:0): You read.
Bloom: Read?
Gia: Read that magazine. You read that magazine.

These expansions of idea, the slowing down of speech, careful enunciation—the total clarification process—indicate the eagerness of children to communicate clearly. Children will usually go to a good deal of trouble to be understood.

It is often the case with siblings that an older child will try to help another person understand the younger one. I have many examples of this. One follows:

(Fred (7:4) and Leslie (3:11) had visited a bakery where they watched the baker decorating a child's birthday cake.)

Leslie: Know what we saw . . .
Fred (interrupting): Upside down . . .
Leslie: What it called with a red . . . suit?
Weeks: *Hmmm?*
Leslie: *Somebody . . . somebody told us that guy with the red suit . . .*
Weeks: *With the red suit?*
Leslie: *Yeah.*
Fred: *Red Riding Hood!*
Leslie: *Yeah.*
Weeks: Oh, Red Riding Hood.

As we noted, children are usually willing to spend considerable effort to make themselves understood, but Leslie was something of an exception to this rule. Because she was more difficult to understand than most children, she was asked to repeat, clarify, or confirm more utterances than most children. When she was younger and had few effective strategies for making herself understood, she often indicated that a guess was correct even when it wasn't. I found this out later by listening carefully to the tape recording, at which time I could often understand utterances that had not been clear to me at the time. Other times she was patient about repeating, as she did in the case of repeating *box* (in Chapter 3) not only to clarify it for me, but in an effort to perfect her own pronunciation of the word. As she got older (and perhaps felt that she was, in fact, speaking understandably) she often became impatient with requests for clarification, for example:

Weeks: What are you drawing?
Leslie (3:7): m duck. /kaɪ/ a duck. (A duck. A kind of
    a duck.)
Weeks: A duck?
Leslie: /i kain/ a duck. Mad duck. (This kind of a duck. Mad
    duck.)
Weeks: What kind of a duck?
Leslie: I can't tell you cause you keep talking! A mad duck!

In spite of her pique, she did repeat, more loudly!

Differences may be expected in the way children respond to requests for clarification, etc., particularly at early ages. Garvey found that the youngest group of children she observed (from 2:10 to 3:3) failed to respond to 40 percent of the contingent queries directed to them by their peers. This would probably have been a somewhat lower figure if it were between children and adults.

One of the things that is interesting about these interruptions in the conversation (requests for clarification, confirmation, etc.) is that speakers respect it as such (an interruption), and as soon as the misunderstanding is taken care of, the conversation resumes as though it had not happened. That is, the person asking for clarification does not take this as an opportunity to assume a turn in conversation that was not due, or to change the topic, etc. The original speaker resumes his or her turn once the misunderstanding is repaired.

Corsaro[38] suggests that the adults' requests for clarification help the child develop competence in communication skills. It has often been said that children communicate poorly in some instances because they fail to offer background cues—they assume adult listeners know more than they do about what the child has on his mind. Corsaro suggests, "With adults' continual request for clarification the child may come to see that interactive contributions are not always as obvious to the hearer as they are to the speaker."

Requests for clarification may indeed serve as subtle lessons to the children on how to make themselves better understood.

Interruptions   It does not seem reasonable to assume that a person can "own" a piece of a conversation, but conversationalists behave as though such rights of ownership do exist. When someone is speaking, others usually respect their right to their turn until it is given up voluntarily. When someone does interrupt, it is treated as an error, a defect in the conversation, even though trivial.

At what age do children become aware of the "right" to a turn—the right to finish speaking without interruption? Anyone who has been around young children very much knows that children seem to interrupt conversations frequently. However, the interruptions by children that most adults are aware of are interruptions in conversations between adults, not conversations in which the child is a partner. For example, the parents are talking to each other, and the child says, "I want a drink of water!" Mother says, "You're interrupting!" In this case, the child was not a party to turn taking in the first place. He was an onlooker, not a participant, and his interruption as such is a part of social behavior but is not part of learning how to take turns in a conversation in which one is a partner.

Motivation for speaking is an important aspect of interruptions. As was pointed out in the section on Early-Language Conversations, even adults have difficulty waiting for the speaker to finish when they have something they desperately want to say. Adults often interrupt under such circumstances. Most of us never reach an age when we are such perfect conversationalists that we *never* interrupt.

In examining my data on children's conversations, I find that children interrupt each other most often in arguing or when one child says something the other objects to:

> Greg (7:4): Jennie's here waiting for her turn to talk and
>   John's sitting here dancing and reading a book . . .
> John (10:11) (interrupting): I'm *not* dancing . . .

On the other hand, when a child has said something wrong, or made a mistake, children of this age wait for a break in the conversation to make the correction, rather than interrupting. Jefferson[39] offers a nice example:

> (Steven, 6:0, Susan, 8:0, and Nancy, 8:0, are playing a game called "Marco Polo" in a swimming pool. The person who is It closes his eyes and the others swim to another position. At the ten-count, It keeps his eyes closed and attempts to locate the others by the sound of their voices as they call "Polo!" As Steven begins to count to ten, Susan and Nancy move to about halfway across the pool.)

> Steven: One, two, three (pause), four, five, six (pause),
>   eleven, eight, nine, ten.
> Susan: Eleven?—eight, nine, ten?
> Steven: Eleven, eight, nine, ten.
> Nancy: E*l*even?
> Steven: Seven, eight, nine, ten.
> Susan: That's better.

From the point of view of the game, the substitution of *eleven* for *seven* was irrelevant. The girls had the same amount of time to move away. Jefferson calls the interchange beyond Steven's counting a *side sequence*. It is a diversion in the game, and in the ongoing activity, much like the requests for clarification discussed above. In this case, however, what is interesting is that Susan (Steven's sister) waited until after he had said *ten* and paused before correcting him. She did not interrupt. He was not offending either of the girls in a personal way, of course, as Greg was John, in the example above.

A surprisingly large number of what may seem to be interruptions in my data turn out not to be even though they are examples of two persons speaking at the same time. In the following example, Fred and Leslie and I were having lunch as the tape recorder was operating. There was only the sound of eating for about two minutes. Then at the same moment, Fred and Leslie both began to talk:

> Fred (7:4): About these guys . . .
> Leslie (3:11): Know what? I saw you (unintelligible)
> Weeks: OK
> Leslie: Today, ummm . . . I . . . um . . .
> Fred: You interrupted me!

When Fred realized they were both talking, he stopped, but Leslie did not. It might be thought that she had not yet learned to defer to the other speaker in such a situation, but within a week of this conversation, Leslie demonstrated she was aware of such rules. Leslie and I had been discussing her new school.

> Weeks: How do you like it?
> Leslie (3:11): Well, good.
> Weeks: You like it good, huh?
> Leslie: What . . .
> Weeks: What kind . . . what?

> Leslie: Well, you start what you was . . . started . . .
> Weeks: What?
> Leslie: You start . . . say what you started to say. OK?

In this case Leslie started talking a fraction of a second before I did, but she deferred to me. Children are much less apt to defer to another child than to an adult in such a situation.

There does not appear to be a dramatic development from childhood to adulthood in the matter of interruptions. As a child becomes better adjusted socially, interruptions become more scarce. Children seem to observe some set of rules regarding the appropriateness of when to talk from earliest ages on, but even as adults, they continue to break these rules by interrupting when strong feelings are aroused. There is less developmental change here, perhaps, than in many other aspects of conversational skills.

Again, a word of warning should be inserted that the discussion applies to the mainstream culture of the United States. Other behaviors are found in other cultures. As Philips[40] says of the American Indians on the Warm Springs Indian Reservation in Oregon,[41] "Indian speakers control the length of their own turns. They are not interrupted. They are rarely cut off by the sudden inattention of selected addressees, primarily because address is so often general." We find quite a different set of conversational rules in operation here. Indian speakers do not select the next speaker by gaze direction (where there is more than one conversational partner), and it is not obligatory to answer questions. A careful examination of my conversations with Yakima Indian children revealed that they interrupted me less often and answered questions less often than did a similar number of non-Indian children of the same age. Whereas many of the non-Indian children would guess at answers and go to any length to avoid saying "I don't know," the Yakima children either said they didn't know, or simply refused to guess, and remained silent.

Remaining Silent   To speak or not to speak? That is the question. At what age do children learn to remain silent when they are supposed to? Piaget[42] says, "Apart from thinking by images or autistic symbols which cannot be directly communicated, the child up to an age as yet undetermined, but probably somewhere about seven, is incapable of keeping to himself the thoughts which enter his mind. He says everything. He has no verbal continence." Mothers of young children tend to believe this fervently. Most children have a difficult time learning when not to talk. However, I have not found age seven to be even close to the age at which the children I know learn to remain silent. There is a great variation in their ability to refrain from talking, but it is before seven.

From about ages two to four, Fred often blurted out such remarks as "You're fat," to a visitor in our home, and asked in a loud voice regarding a thin man standing close to us, "Is that man a scarecrow?" Fred's propensity to make such remarks more frequently than the other five children was partly due, I suppose, to the fact that he talked more than the other children. He was also much slower in learning to use a whisper in situations that required it. While the other children began to whisper occasionally almost as soon as they learned to talk, Fred was about four when he was first heard whispering a secret. At 4:6 Fred had just helped to buy and wrap a gadget bag for his father's birthday when he went into a store with his parents, and his father picked up a gadget bag identical to the one already purchased, and admired it. Fred watched silently, but only a few months earlier he would certainly have informed his father that they had already gotten him one.

In this case, and many similar occasions, it is desirable to keep quiet. In other kinds of situations, silence is uncomfortable, at least in our culture. Long silences are usually comfortably tolerated between family members, and in general in a living situation, where a pause can be interpreted as the end of a given conversation, even though the participants remain in the same physical positions (as at the dinner table). However, in other situations, long pauses become awkward, and "small talk" has been devised to fill in the gaps. A good deal of conversation thus turns out to be asking questions that the speaker doesn't really want to know the answer to, and discussing trivia.

Again, this is not the case with Yakima Indians or with Warm Springs Indians. Philips[43] says, "The pauses between two different speakers' turns at talk are frequently longer than is the case in Anglo interactions. There is a tolerance for silences—silences that Anglos often rush into and fill."

As was mentioned in the section on Early-Language Conversations, John filled in pauses in adult conversation[44] with "a door." Beginning at 2:11 he filled pauses in adult conversations with more appropriate remarks. For example, his grandparents had picked him and his parents up at the airport, and while his grandfather waited to pay the toll at the airport parking lot, he commented. "Sure is a nice car." "Sure is a nice _____" was one of his most frequently used comments during a conversational lull.

Hymes[45] has pointed out that "A child capable of any and all grammatical utterances, but not knowing which to use, not knowing even when to talk and when to stop, would be a cultural monstrosity." I know no cultural monstrosities. Children learn rather quickly (not as quickly as we might like, however) not to say whatever they happen to be thinking on some occasions, and to figure out something appropriate to say on other occasions, and they sort out such occasions at an earlier age than many researchers (such as Piaget) have previously led us to believe.

Choice of Partners

To whom can a child talk? In our culture, almost anyone. In some cultures, a child may not have such a free choice of partners. In some places, a child is to speak only when spoken to. This was more generally true in the United States in the past than it is now. Many researchers have shown clearly that when two or three children of approximately the same age are put in a room of toys together, they converse with each other. It is usually assumed that children of the same age will be considered appropriate conversational partners. Beyond that it is a question of whether or not individuals of other ages are appropriate, whether or not strangers may be freely addressed, and what effect the setting and proximity will have on the determination of partners.

In Chapter 3 it is noted that Jennie (2:11) initiated (albeit nonverbally) a conversation with an old man who sat down on a bench beside her at the Department of Motor Vehicles, and later with a woman (verbally this time) in the same place. The six children I regularly observe are accustomed to having frequent conversation with adult members of the family as well as with a wide variety of other adults. In some homes, adults do not consider children suitable conversational partners, and such children are probably less inclined to initiate conversations with adults they do not know. Harkness[46] observed rural Spanish-speaking Guatemalan children aged 1:6 to 3:6 and their mothers, and reports, "Some of the children that I observed interacted predominantly with other children, while their mothers only occasionally interjected a command or prohibition. One mother frankly told me, 'I never talk with my child. I just tell him to do something and he does it. When he talks, it's with other children.' " Such attitudes are not limited to Guatemala; they are found in homes, principally lower socioeconomic homes, in this country as well. It is predictable that children from such homes will have more difficulty maintaining a conversation with other adults, such as classroom teachers, than a child who is considered an interesting conversational partner by adults in his own family.

The setting plays an important role in determining with whom a child will converse. Hymes[47] reports that a Russian visitor to France was astonished when the children of his host remained silent at the dinner table; Russian children would have been scolded for *not* joining in the conversation with a guest. Hymes does not say how old these children were. In American homes, children under three years of age, for example, are seldom expected to join in any conversation. Likewise, children rarely seem to want to. They may want the attention of the adults who are conversing, but it is not usual for a child of that age to be expected to sit quietly and attend to the conversation of adults or enter into it. (John did do this, however, and I consider him to be an exception to the rule). In middle-class homes, at least, older children are expected to join in dinner-table conversations. Generally, any guest in the home is fair game for conversations among the children I know. The same is true for homes of friends, or social occasions in places other than the home, such as clubs or restaurants.

Public places intended for recreation, such as parks, are also places where strangers usually free feel to converse. It was noted earlier that Fred initiated a conversation with a boy older than himself in a children's park. This is not the case in places of business, such as an airport or a hotel lobby, for example. Nor would one expect to find a conversational partner at the Department of Motor Vehicles, as happened with Jennie. The determining factor in this case was the proximity of the persons involved; these two older persons sat on a bench directly beside Jennie. Likewise, on a train or bus, one may strike up a conversation with one's seatmate. One does not stop a stranger on a city street for conversation. Fred, however, at 4:9 spoke to older children whom he did not know passing his home in the suburbs. One's own neighborhood, as an extension of the home, is a place where one may speak to strangers.

It may be seen, then, that while there are some restrictions as to where a child may initiate a conversation, there are few restrictions as to whom a child may talk; certainly age, race, and sex offer no barriers where the average middle-class child is concerned (though a child may initiate a conversation much more rapidly with another person of the same sex and similar age and race). It may also be seen that children whose early language experiences have been chiefly with peers in a neighborhood setting (as opposed to a wide variety of conversational partners in a wide variety of settings) may have difficulty talking to teachers and other adults during later periods such as school years.

Topic

What can children talk about, either among themselves or with adults? What topics are possible and appropriate? Examination of transcripts or peer conversations reveals that children usually talk about their ongoing activities. They are busy with toys or books, or are engaged in role-playing activities, etc., and discussion centers on what they are doing. It is rarely the case that children just sit and converse in the way adults do. When children's conversation stop focusing on objects, it often reverts to nonsense, as reported by Keenan.[48] At 2:9, her twin sons were tape-recorded during early morning hours in their beds. She reports that the nonsense, as well as the sensible speech, was largely directed to the other child, as opposed to being egocentric. So simply having fun with language can serve children in lieu of a more "proper" topic of conversation.

One of the reasons adults have some difficulty in finding a topic of conversation when faced with a child is that the adult is not prepared to play games with the child and the child is not accustomed to talking about events removed in time and space. Requests for demographic information, such as name and age, do not take a conversation very far. A child can talk, however, about what he is doing or has done in the past. Sometimes children want to talk about such things and are not given the chance. For example:

Weeks: What did you do yesterday at school?
Leslie (4:7): I listened to a story. Was a horse. And roses maked him sneeze. And his nose itched and his eyes itched. Sumpin' else. I had ... uh I haved ... a had a motorcycle and I sit down and thinking what I was doing and lookin' at all those kids and teacher goed by and she didn't ask me anything.
Weeks: What might she have asked you?
Leslie: How come you're sittin' here?

Although adults have a limited number of topics they can think of to introduce with children, the children I work with almost always have topics they want to discuss when I ask them. And I frequently do. In part, it is an exercise in getting them to talk about something other than ongoing activities, and I have found that during such conversations, their language is significantly different—sentences are longer and more complex and the vocabulary is more varied. Some of the topics they introduce include: (1) Their own past. They like to reminisce about things they used to do (even at 3½ or 4!), some of which have been told to them by adults, and others which they have remembered independently upon being reminded of incidents they had forgotten. (2) My past. I tell them stories of when I was a child, and it stimulates them to tell their own experiences of a similar nature. (3) Their dreams. At 6:0, Jennie spent about half an hour telling me about her dreams and nightmares, and asking for explanations about questions that arose as a result of them, such as "A dog could eat a cat?" (She has two cats.) And "Are there really monsters?" (4) School activities. A popular topic. (5) Future activities. "What are we going to do this afternoon?" They enjoy talking about what they want to do before they do it. (6) Imaginary things. "Would it be fun to live in a haunted house?" This was Gregory's question (3:7) and he enjoyed talking about a make-believe world.

This is not an exhaustive list, but it suggests that children are able to talk about a wide range of topics, even at early ages.

When children "initiate" a conversation, however, as discussed earlier, this usually consists of a greeting, or getting the attention of the addressee, and making some kind of request or giving the adult an opportunity to introduce a topic. The topics I discussed above were introduced because I asked the children for suggestions. This is not routine in conversations ("I would like to talk to you if you have something you want to talk about."). My situation was unique in that I approached the children with a task: we were to talk for half an hour, or an hour; we could talk about my topic or theirs.[49]

Compliments   Children begin learning to make judgments about what is appropriate to say at about the same time they begin talking. Appropriateness plays an important role in compliments. Children must learn what they may offer compliments about and what they may not. In the Arabic-speaking population of the Northern Sudan, one may ask a woman what kind of work her husband does but must not ask what her husband's name is; one may ask a child his name and age but must not make admiring comments on his health, size, or appearance.[50]

The children I observe have learned more quickly to give compliments than to receive them graciously. With the exception of Brandon (1:6) and Kara (0:8), all of the children have been heard giving their mothers compliments regarding their hair, clothes, or general appearance, patterned (sometimes word for word) after what they hear their fathers say. At age five, Leslie said to her mother, "You're a cute little mommy!" and to her grandfather, "You're sweet!" Jennie was the most lavish with compliments. She started at 2:7 watching while her mother dressed to go out, making remarks such as "Oh! Pretty!" and "Oh! Sweet." Fred, John, and Gregory were all inclined to give their younger siblings frequent compliments, principally about their clothes or general appearance. Before Leslie was a year old, Fred (4:3) started commenting to her about new dresses, hair ribbons, etc. When Leslie was 1:5 she was wearing a new dress for the first time when Fred came in from play. She stood waiting for him to comment, but he walked past without noticing her. She followed him until he stopped and she touched him on the stomach and said "Uh" (her word for "Notice!"). He was busy and still didn't look at her. She waited a second and she hit him on the stomach and said "Uh" louder and pulled her skirt out in front. He finally looked at her and said, "Oh, you have on a new dress!" She laughed aloud and twisted around a little, her hands on her dress, to show her appreciation for the nice compliment. By the time Fred was nine and Leslie was six, compliments had become so sparse that Fred's remark to Leslie, "You're a really nice little sister," moved her to tears. This, however, seems to be the norm in our culture. At later ages again, both boys and girls give compliments more frequently, but to nonsiblings.

The children had also learned that it was appropriate to compliment the cook on a meal, or any food offered. Each of the children learned (independently, it seemed) to compliment me most lavishly on food they didn't actually like. I gave Jennie a mixture of some nuts, raisins, dried fruits, etc., from a bowl when she was 2:8. She took some, ate it, and said, "Mmmmm, wuv it!" but she could not be persuaded to have a second bite! I suppose they think I will not be so offended when they don't eat it if they have offered a compliment about it. These compliments seemed to reveal an awareness of how another person's feelings might be affected by what they said.

Changing the Topic   We all learn how to change the topic when we become bored with it, are ignorant on the topic, or have thought of one that shows us up in a better light. We probably learned to do this almost as soon as we learned how to talk. By 2:5, in response to a question he couldn't or didn't want to answer, John resorted to simply talking about something else, often something very inconsequential. He would hardly take a breath in order to prevent the question he didn't want to answer from being asked again.

By 3:0 Fred often relied on a "stall tactic" while trying to think of a good answer to an adult's question. He would say "Oh," with a falling intonation and pause as though he were ready to go on with his answer. If an answer didn't come readily to mind, he might repeat the "Oh" four or five times. If he hadn't thought of an answer by then, he would resort to changing the subject. He would never admit he didn't know the answer or voluntarily give up his turn in conversation. At 3:4, for example, I was showing him pictures and asking him to make up a story about what was happening in the picture. One picture baffled him and after two oh's he said, "We could have a little visit." I said, "All right. What shall we visit about?" and that was his opportunity to introduce a topic of his own choosing.

By 5:0, Leslie had learned to say, "Oh, talking of that . . ." and then introduce an entirely new subject in much the same way adults do, while trying to conceal the fact that they are changing the subject. "By the way," "That reminds me" are also used to signal a change of topic.

Gregory had the least devious method of all. He usually stated simply, "I don't want to talk about that." When the adult answered, "Well, what would you like to talk about?" Gregory had a ready answer.

In summary, children talk principally among themselves on the topic of their ongoing activities. This is also a possible topic for interaction with adults, though possible topics between children and adults are wide-ranging. Children also learn between ages two and three to give appropriate compliments to individuals they know well. (I have no examples of children offering compliments to strangers.) Children's skill in conversing with adults and in giving compliments depends heavily on participation in such activities at home. By this same age, children learn how to change topics that are not to their liking.

Telephone Conversations

Telephones are standard equipment in middle-class homes in the United States and Canada,[51] and children learn at very early ages to talk on play telephones, patterning their conversations after those they hear. At 1:4 Brandon began holding "conversations" on his toy telephone using babbling with sentence intonation patterns interspersed with a great deal of laughing. His telephone babbling was even somewhat lower in volume (much as adult voices are) than his other babbling.

There are many communication patterns that are unique to telephone conversations. Individuals ordinarily answer the telephone differently than they greet anyone in person. The initial greeting when one is answering the telephone cannot be varied to suit the listener because at this point, the speaker does not know who it is that has called him. Leslie was heard many times answering her play telephone with "eh o o" using an intonation pattern her mother used in answering the phone, but exaggerating it. Leslie was not heard using this intonation pattern any other time (nor was her mother, for that matter), nor did Leslie use the greeting "Hello." "Hi" was her standard greeting in person. Ervin-Tripp and Mitchell-Kernan[52] suggest that a typical two-year-old telephone conversation may be "Hi. Fine. Bye," consisting only of what have been called *routines*.

To compensate for the lack of eye contact and other nonverbal aspects of communication, more verbal affirmation that one is receiving the message is usually given on the telephone than in person—the listener says "yes," or "um hmmm," more often. Leslie's conversations up to age 3:0 or so consisted almost entirely of "um hmmm"s. She always seemed to be listening.

Crystal and Davy[53] point out that silences tend to be reduced in length in telephone conversation because silence is often interpreted as a breakdown of communication ("Hello? Are you there?") or as an opportunity to interrupt. Since play telephone conversations involve only one person, such distinctions cannot be noted, even if the child is sophisticated enough to make them. However, Ervin-Tripp has studied some real telephone conversations between children (3:6) and reports the following sequence (Ervin-Tripp and Mitchell-Kernan[54]):

A:	Makes funny noises.
B:	Deliberately drops phone, giggles, while—
A:	Giggles and sings.
B:	Tells nonsense about animals, giggles, while—
A:	Calls B silly billy and funny bunny.
B:	Pretends to be a dog, barks, while—
A:	Sings.
B:	Says bye, then says hi, asserts he was kidding, tricking.
A:	Fantasies wild trip, while—
B:	Mixes up nursery rhymes.
A:	Does nonsense sound play, then sings, while—
B:	Tries to get the floor for a nursery rhyme joke.
A and B:	Both participate in making funny endings for nursery rhymes, alternating turns.

Again we see that where there is no ongoing physical activity (the children are separated in space), language play can serve in lieu of a more traditional topic of conversation. No silences are reported here; rather there is overlapping of vocalizing. The authors continue:

Play makes salient a dimension of variation between genres: the roles of partner and audience. The phone sequence above provides an example of a contrast between two types of turn-taking patterns, both typical of play. In the shared task of making funny endings for nursery rhymes, the initiator made a clear attempt to recover from interruption and demand the floor, and the two engaged in turn-taking. The turn-taking sequence, however, was preceded by another pattern, in which productions could be simultaneous, less focused partner attention was allowed, and only a sharing of key was needed. In this modality, each partner becomes a stimulus to the play of the other but neither requires proof of full attention.

Children who are exposed to adult telephone conversations learn to produce quite realistically one side of a make-believe conversation on a toy telephone usually before their second birthday. For most children, learning to carry on a real conversation on a real telephone comes much later. The example offered by Ervin-Tripp and Mitchell-Kernan suggests that early real telephone conversations may be situations in which children feel free to talk simultaneously while indulging in language play, as opposed to necessarily taking turns.

Monologues

A monologue is a long speech uttered by one person while in company with others. While the person giving a monologue does not seek an exchange of ideas, and does not offer the listener an opportunity for a turn at speaking, according to this definition, a monologue does require a listener. The speaker may be very responsive to the nonverbal responses of the listener, such as facial expressions, even though the listener is given no chance to respond verbally. Piaget[55] classified a monologue as a variety of egocentric speech. Because Piaget's terminology has caused considerable confusion, it will be discussed briefly here. Piaget's three categories of egocentric speech include: (1) *Repetition* (*echolalia*). He includes here only the repetition of words and syllables which a child repeats for the pleasure of hearing them. He maintains that this is a "remnant of baby prattle, obviously devoid of any social character." (2) *Monologue.* Piaget describes this, "The child talks to himself as though he were thinking aloud. He does not address anyone." (3) *Dual or collective monologue.* "The contradiction contained in the phrase recalls the paradox of those conversations between children which we were discussing, where an outsider is always associated with the action or thought of the moment, but is expected neither to attend nor to understand. The point of view of the other person is never taken into account; his presence serves only as a stimulus."

Much of what Piaget included as egocentric speech is currently recognized as serving a social function. Even the repetition of words and syllables, classified now as language play, often serves a social role, as is pointed out in Chapter 3. Even when children are talking to themselves about their own ongoing activities, Vygotsky[56] has shown that the amount of talking diminishes dramatically when the child knows that no one is listening. He performed several experiments, one in which children were in a situation where there were either deaf-mute children or children speaking a foreign language; a second in which the children were either with strangers or were entirely alone; the third in which there was music playing nearby that was so loud it drowned out the voices of the children and others in the room; or a situation in which the children were forbidden to talk loudly and allowed to talk only in whispers. In all these situations "egocentric" speech disappeared or was greatly reduced. This suggests that, while children did not expect to take turns speaking and listening, they did expect to be heard and understood.

Monologues most often accompany children's play activities at young ages, but as children get older, they may use such speech in other situations where they are confident of an attentive listener. In the case of Jennie's monologue below, both Greg and I were listeners, and Greg was waiting rather impatiently to talk.

> Jennie (5:0): And today we have a talk . . . a newstalk . . . and today Greg was just doing that, so bye bye, and today, um, we like to . . . um . . . Grandma was smiling and she gave me a bottle of perfume . . . um . . . in the morning that was really nice from her, and . . . and today Grandma was just sitting here and she's giving me a bottle of perfume. She was really nice giving me that to keep, and she . . . she giving me a tray with a mirror, and taking it back. That was really nice, too. And today Grandpa's out campus and we saw them and we went to the store and we went to a library and we had a really big day doing that, and we really was just doing fooling-around stuff, and Grandma gave us a piece of gum in the car . . . that was very nice. We didn't say thank you yet, but I said it on the microphone. But she was gonna tape just really nice for us. She said, "Why don't you play nurse, or watch TV?" but we decided that we wanted to talk in the microphone and we was gonna decide talking on the microphone. And I was coloring on . . . um . . . Pinocchio book, whatever it's called and um . . . and . . .

Jennie watched my face for reassurance that she could continue talking, and some of the repetitions and fillers ("um") seemed to be for the purpose of preventing Greg from talking.

Anthony Weir's bedtime soliloquies[57] have sometimes been called monologues, but they are clearly egocentric speech inasmuch as Anthony was alone in his room and had no knowledge of the hidden microphone. His speech is discussed in Chapter 3.

It may be seen that Piaget considered monologues to be directed toward oneself without an audience (egocentric speech), while the definition I am using assumes an audience for monologues.

Summary

Conversation, a matter of alternate talking and listening between at least two individuals, is something children learn to engage in at a very early age. Conversation-like behavior begins as early as eight or nine weeks of age with infants exchanging vocalizations in a turn-taking fashion with their mothers. Long before children have learned what to say in a conversation, they have learned something about when and how to say it.

Greetings, often a prelude to conversation, are universal in human speech communities. Greetings and farewells (*hi* and *bye-bye*) are among the earliest language forms learned by children. By age two or three, perhaps earlier, children greet persons of different ages and persons in different roles in different ways. More deference is given to older persons, for example.

A greeting sometimes serves as a "summons" for the right to talk, particularly when children wish to talk to adults. "Know what?" is also used in this way sometimes. Once a speaker has the attention of a listener, a question is the most common way to start a conversation. When both speaker and hearer are children of the same age, it may be expected that questions and answers will be somewhat evenly distributed between them. It has been found, however, that when teachers converse with primary-age children, they control the conversation with successive questions (and few answers).

Recent research regarding children's ability to make and respond to requests of various kinds indicates that children differentiate at an early age between the appropriate form of directives intended for peers, strange or familiar adults, and situations where the request is likely to be complied with or not. For example, polite forms are used when addressing adults or children who may refuse the request, and imperatives are directed to peers or to younger children. The social sophistication of a child seems to have more bearing on his or her ability to interpret (and use) indirect requests (including hints) than intelligence or language development per se.

Children also learn how to make, and respond appropriately to, requests for clarification when they are not sure they have understood correctly, and request more information when that which they have been given appears inadequate. In these cases, they recognize that such a request and the response is a digression in the conversation, and when it is over, the conversation reverts to the original turn-taking of the speaker and listener. (Such a break in the conversation is not used to take a turn that was not due the child.) When such misunderstandings take place, older siblings are often eager to help clarify the situation.

Children, just like adults, interrupt their conversational partners most often when the partner has said something they object to, consider insulting, etc. Children are aware of the proprieties of turn taking and most often break the rules when their feelings are aroused.

Some children, such as John, learn before age three to make appropriate "small talk" and fill in gaps in a conversation. This may be partly to avoid the embarrassment of silence in a conversation, and partly to assert their standing as a conversational partner (or to assert their position as a member of the adult group).

It is assumed that in any culture a child's own peers will be considered appropriate conversational partners. It is also generally the case that it is appropriate for one to initiate a conversation with a person younger than oneself. In the mainstream American culture, age is no barrier to conversation in most situations—a child may initiate a conversation with persons of any age if the setting is appropriate (home or neighborhood, for example). It is also the case that children in the mainstream American culture may initiate conversations with persons of either sex or of any ethnic group, but this is not universally true. In this culture there are few conversational taboos, and children may talk with conversational partners on any topic about which they have a bit of knowledge. The children I have observed have learned almost as soon as they learned to talk to offer appropriate compliments to family members. They sometimes receive compliments with embarrassment, however. Figure 1 depicts some of the ways in which children learn to interact with others appropriately in various settings.

Monologues, which do not involve turn taking but which do require a listener (differentiating them from egocentric speech), are observed from early ages on.

Child sees his teacher in grocery store: "Good morning, Mrs. Mayberry!" (To others: "Hi!")

"You're a nice mommy to give me some of your coke."

To new acquaintance: "Would you please help me up?" (To younger brother: "Help me!")

Figure 1   Children learn at an early age to give compliments, make requests, and offer greetings appropriately according to: (1) age, (2) familiarity, (3) role, (4) setting, and (5) occasion.

In general, conversational skills are developed in the mainstream American culture at a much earlier age than has previously been indicated by the literature, principally European, on child language development.

NOTES

1. Crystal, David, and Derek Davy. *Investigating English Style*, Bloomington, Ind.: Indiana University Press, 1969.

2. *Ibid.*, p. 104.

3. Chomsky, Noam. *Aspects of the Theory of Syntax*, Cambridge, Mass.: MIT Press, 1965, pp. 31, 201.

4. Hymes, Dell H. "The Ethnography of Speaking," in *Readings in the Sociology of Language*, edited by Joshua A. Fishman, The Hague: Mouton, 1968, p. 111.

5. Trevarthen, Colwyn. "Conversations with a Two-Month-Old," *New Scientist*, May 2, 1974, 230-235.

6. Freedle, Roy, and Michael Lewis. "Prelinguistic Conversations," in *Interaction, Conversation, and the Development of Language*, edited by Michael Lewis and Leonard A. Rosenblum, New York: Wiley, 1977.

7. *Ibid.*, p. 158.

8. Gleason, Jean Berko, and Sandra Weintraub. "The Acquisition of Routines in Child Language," *Language in Society*, 1976, 5:129-136.

9. Ferguson, Charles A. "The Structure and Use of Politeness Formulas," *Language in Society*, 1976, 5:137-151.

10. *Ibid.*

11. Schegloff, Emanuel A. "Notes on a Conversational Practice: Formulating Place," in *Studies in Social Interaction*, edited by David Sudnow, New York: Free Press, 1972.

12. This is discussed from a slightly different point of view by Matthew Speier (*How to Observe Face-to-Face Communication: A Sociological Introduction*, Pacific Palisades, Calif.: Goodyear Publishing Co., 1973). He suggests that children have a culture of their own, and refers to the proximity of the adult culture as that of culture contact. Children thus do not have the same access to adults that adults do to children or to other adults. This approach suggests that it is not just children's ineptness with language that determines, for example, what form of summons they will use, but what form a child (as opposed to an adult) *must* use in order to establish a conversation.

13. Scollon, Ronald. *Conversations with a One Year Old*, Hawaii: University Press of Hawaii, 1976, p. 124.

14. *Ibid.*, p. 128.

15. Garvey, Catherine, and R. Hogan. "Social Speech and Social Interaction: Egocentrism Revisited," *Child Development*, 1973, 44:562-568.

16. Mishler, Elliot G. "Studies in Dialogue and Discourse: An Exponential Law of Successive Questioning," *Language in Society*, 1975, 4:31-51, and "Studies in Dialogue and Discourse: II. Types of Discourse Initiated by and Sustained through Questioning," *Journal of Psycholinguistic Research*, 1975, 4:99-121.

17. Ervin-Tripp, Susan M., and Wick Miller. "Early Discourse: Some Questions about Questions," in *Interaction, Conversation, and the Development of Language*, edited by Michael Lewis and Leonard A. Rosenblum, New York: Wiley, 1977, p. 14.

18. Goffman, Erving. *Interactional Ritual*, Garden City, N.Y.: Doubleday, 1967.

19. Ervin-Tripp, Susan M. "Early Discourse Patterns," paper presented at Stanford Child Language Seminar, May 28, 1975.

20. Garvey, Catherine. "Requests and Responses in Children's Speech," *Journal of Child Language*, 1975, 2:41-63.

21. Mueller, Edward. "The Maintenance of Verbal Exchanges between Young Children," *Child Development*, 1972, 43:930-938.

22. Piaget, Jean. *The Language and Thought of the Child*, New York: Meridian Books, 1955 (first published in 1926).

23. Glucksberg, Sam, Robert M. Krauss, and Robert Weisberg. "Referential Communication in Nursery School Children: Method and Some Preliminary Findings," *Journal of Experimental Child Psychology*, 1966, 3:333-342.

24. Ervin-Tripp, Susan M. *Language Acquisition and Communicative Choice*, Stanford, Calif.: Stanford University Press, 1973; "Is Sybil There? The Structure of Some American English Directives," *Language in Society*, 1976, 5:25-66; and "Wait for Me, Roller Skate!" in *Child Discourse*, edited by Susan Ervin-Tripp and Claudia Mitchell-Kernan, New York: Academic Press, 1977.

25. Garvey, Catherine. "Requests and Responses in Children's Speech," *Journal of Child Language*, 1975, 2:41-63.

26. Dore, John. "Communicative Intentions and Pragmatic Strategies in the Conversations of Preschool Children," mimeographed paper, April 1975.

27. "Wait for Me, Roller Skate!"

28. *Op. cit.,* p. 42.

29. "Wait for Me, Roller Skate!" p. 166.

30. *Ibid.,* p. 179.

31. Dore, John. "Oh Them Sheriff," in *Child Discourse.*

32. Shatz, Marilyn. "On the Development of Communicative Understandings: An Early Strategy for Interpreting and Responding to Messages," in *Studies in Social and Cognitive Development*, edited by J. Glick and A. Clarke-Stewart, New York: Gardner Press, 1977.

33. "Wait for Me, Roller Skate!" pp. 183-184.

34. Lawson, Craig. "Request Patterns in a Two-Year-Old," unpublished manuscript, Berkeley, Calif., 1967.

35. MacWhinney, Brian. "Some Observations on Requests by Hungarian Children," unpublished manuscript, Denver, Colo., 1974.

36. Garvey, Catherine. "The Contingent Query: A Dependent Act in Conversation," in *Interaction, Conversation, and the Development of Language.*

37. Bloom, Lois, Peggy Miller, and Lois Hood. "Variation and Reduction as Aspects of Competence in Language Development," in *The 1974 Minnesota Symposia on Child Psychology*, edited by A. Pick, Minneapolis: University of Minnesota Press, 1977.

38. Corsaro, William A. "The Clarification Request as a Feature of Adult Interactive Styles with Young Children," *Language in Society*, 1977, 6:183-207.

39. Jefferson, Gail. "Side Sequences," in *Studies in Social Interaction.*

40. Philips, Susan U. "Some Sources of Cultural Variability in the Regulation of Talk," *Language in Society*, 1976, 5:81-95.

41. The Warm Springs Indian Reservation is located in central Oregon just south of the Columbia River, not far from the Yakima Indian Reservation in central Washington. The older Yakima Indians, as well as many of the older Warm Springs Indians, speak Sahaptin, their native Indian language.

42. *The Language and Thought of the Child*, p. 59.

43. *Op. cit.*, p. 88.

44. I judge that he considered himself a full conversational partner even though the adults involved did not think of him in that way—they were not addressing any speech directly to him.

45. Hymes, Dell H. "Models of the Interaction of Language and Social Setting," *Journal of Social Issues*, 1967, 23:8-28, p. 16.

46. Harkness, Sara. "Cultural Variation in Mothers' Language," in *Child Language—1975*, edited by Walburga von Raffler-Engel, International Linguistic Association, 1976. (Special issue of *Word*, 1971, 27:495-498.)

47. "The Ethnography of Speaking," p. 129.

48. Keenan, Elinor O. "Conversational Competence in Children," *Journal of Child Language*, 1974, 1:163-183.

49. I should add here that the children all *loved* to have a chance to have an attentive adult conversational partner for any length of time. One of their most frequent questions was "When are we going to tape?"

50. Griffiths, V. L., and Abdel Rahman All Taha. *Sudan Courtesy Customs*, The Sudan Government, 1936.

51. This is not true, however, in urban ghettos, American Indian Reservations, or some less developed countries. There are currently 145 million telephones (as opposed to 122 million television sets) in the United States and 360 million telephones worldwide (as opposed to 365 million television sets). Many Yakima Indian families with whom I have worked have a television set but no telephone.

52. Ervin-Tripp, Susan M., and Claudia Mitchell-Kernan (eds.). *Child Discourse*, New York: Academic Press, 1977, p. 10.

53. *Investigating English Style*.

54. *Op. cit.*, p. 13.

55. *The Language and Thought of the Child*, p. 32.

56. Vygotsky, L. S. *Thought and Language*, Cambridge, Mass.: MIT Press, 1962.

57. Weir, Ruth Hirsch. *Language in the Crib*, The Hague: Mouton, 1962.

SUGGESTED READINGS

Ervin-Tripp, Susan M., and Claudia Mitchell-Kernan (eds.). *Child Discourse*, New York: Academic Press, 1977.

Lewis, Michael, and Leonard A. Rosenblum (eds.). *Interaction, Conversation, and the Development of Language*, New York: Wiley, 1977.

Scollon, Ronald. *Conversations with a One Year Old*, Hawaii: University Press of Hawaii, 1976.

Speier, Matthew. *How to Observe Face-to-Face Communication: A Sociological Introduction*, Pacific Palisades, Calif.: Goodyear Publishing Co., 1973.

Weir, Ruth Hirsch. *Language in the Crib*, The Hague: Mouton, 1962.

3

Language Play
and Games

Gregory (3:7) had a book and was pretending to read:

"He was very happy, like that picture, he's walking and
he's gonna be bong! he went into a stone and . . . He was
running, he was walking, woop! There was a tail thing and it
bite my tail. He was OK. He was trying . . . there was . . .
there was one by my . . . one by my back. That's good. What
gonna do with that? Where's this going? Bye bye. Don't let
this go. Oooo! Let them go away. It's night! It's night time.
Go to bed if you want to. He started a bubble. Bubble,
bubble, bubble, bubble, pubble, bubble, puggle, puddle. He
started a bubble, He went to a mouth and bubble, puddle,
buddle, buddle, pable, table up on chair. (He pauses to
laugh.) He went to the doctor so he . . . he stop . . . he stop
bubbling. He listened to his heart brup, brup, krup, krip,
krip, bra, bra . . . that house. The doctor house is gonna tip
down. He went to . . . he wasn't stop doing that. Something
is *very* wrong. Something *is* very wrong. Is I tell you
something was wrong? Rain is wrong!"

This example of Greg's "reading" or telling a story from pictures includes many kinds of language play. He made up rhyming words, nonsense words, used sound effects, and at the end, varied the same sentence in three ways: first by using two different stress patterns, then by transforming (albeit incorrectly) the statement to a question. He also repeated *wrong* in the final sentence. He used a wide range of intonation patterns (rising and falling pitch), and varied the speed. He was obviously enjoying himself.

Babbling

Of all possible varieties of language play engaged in by young children, babbling is the most common and has been discussed the most. Lewis[1] says "When a child is babbling he gives us the impression that he is making sounds 'for their own sake,' that he derives satisfaction from the utterance itself, that he is 'playing with sounds,' playing with his vocal organs in the same way as he plays with movements of his fingers and his toes."

Babbling and cooing both begin during the early months of infancy—usually by about the sixth week, and continue beyond the time that real speech begins. Some linguists consider cooing to be the earliest stage of sound production beyond crying, with babbling following, but others, including myself, have observed cooing and babbling during the same period. Although cooing and babbling both take place during periods of contentment, they are distinguished in that cooing is usually thought of as an "expressive" sound because it carries meaning—it is an expression of the child's state of comfort and contentment. Babbling does not express any meaning, though it often appears to be an attempt on the part of the child to communicate. To what extent babbling may be thought of as a "practicing language" and to what extent as merely playing with sounds is a matter that cannot be easily resolved.

While Lenneberg[2] maintains that cooing and babbling do not represent "practice stages for future verbal behavior," and Jakobson[3] calls babbling an articulatory exercise that is unrelated to later speech, recent studies[4] offer evidence that babbling is more than random noise; there *is* a continuity between babbling and meaningful child speech. The presence of an element of learning in the babbling does not prevent it from qualifying as play, however. It is self-initiated and one need only watch babies as they babble to deduce that they are enjoying it.

Of the children whose language development I follow, Fred, John, and Greg, were great babblers and were fast in speech development; Brandon babbled somewhat less, while the girls, Kara, Jennie, and Leslie, babbled very little. Kara is not yet talking, but Jennie and Leslie were slower in speech development than the boys were. Neither the girls nor Brandon were "people imitators" where language was concerned. They didn't enjoy trying to say words or make sounds suggested by someone else, while the other three boys usually responded to this as a game and enjoyed it. Leslie was an imitator of other sounds such as motor noises and animal sounds, but not speech sounds. This lack of pleasure in babbling and imitation games did not appear to be related to a general lack of a sense of humor. All the children delighted in other kinds of play and initiated numerous games of other kinds.

As was mentioned above, Fred and John in particular responded with babbling when a familiar adult talked to them. Fred babbled at great lengths with sentence intonation patterns, and gave the impression that he thought he was responding in kind. John babbled as readily, but with less variation in intonation, when adults talked to him. I observed repeatedly between 0:6 and 0:11 that Greg, who adored John, babbled much more when the two of them were playing than when he was with adults or with other children, suggesting that babbling was an activity that indicated happiness for him. It is also interesting to note here that while John, the first-born child of the family, modeled his speech after his father and made elaborate attempts to use adult words and phrases, Greg modeled his speech, and most of his other behavior, after John. His speech was far less sophisticated at any comparable age than John's.

It may be significant that the girls responded just as readily to adult attention as the boys did, but with either smiles or laughter. In the process of conversation, smiles and laughter are appropriate responses, and we can readily find adults who are more inclined to respond this way in social situations than with speech. Indeed, even at school age (five to nine), Leslie responds much more frequently in conversation with smiles and laughter than Fred does, for example, while Fred and John seldom lack a ready verbal response. I also noticed in peeking in on Leslie when she was alone in her crib from ages 0:5 to about 1:0 that she frequently smiled, laughed, or squealed as she played alone, though she seldom produced speech sounds. Her lack of babbling did not indicate a lack of contentment.

One can only speculate about the relationship between the amount of babbling a baby does and the rate of speech production. I would not expect to find a cause-and-effect relationship, although there may be a correlation and a common cause for lack of babbling and slow speech production. A very small amount of babbling may be considered a predictor, not a cause, of slow speech development during the early language development period.

Norman[5] describes some aspects of the babbling of a nine-month-old girl: "When she heard her own strings of nonsense syllables said to her by her companions, she showed real delight, and was able to repeat these syllables in turn after the adults. In this there seemed to be the first communication in the sense of a give and take of speech-sounds, or of sounds that were later to become speech, and a sharing of pleasure and interest in them." Norman also states that the child showed great satisfaction in being able to produce babbling that was similar to adult speech in intonation.

Leopold reports some of Hildegard's spontaneous language play at age 2:1:[6] "She often sings in a cheerful mood, without a melody, but musically and with a good variety of tones. The underlain words are strangely fixed: /maɪ do we/ with rising notes, *My go away*, and sometimes words from the kitten story, also many babbling syllables without meaning." And at 2:2, Leopold reported "Linguistic games with nonsense syllables, which all observers of child-language report, had not been noticed in Hildegard's case up to now, apart from babbling, of course. During the summer she sometimes sang words the meaning of which had evaporated, stereotype /maɪ do we/ *My go away*. Now she does the same thing at the piano with /maɪ mama ʔɛʃ/ *My Mama is*, repeated several times, which never had any meaning. Once she turned around to me from the piano and said /maɪ mama ʔɛʃ mɔ:/ which has no meaning that I can make out, but shows that she had become conscious of the semantically unsatisfactory character of the words. And then pure nonsense syllables appeared also."

Fluent Nonsense Talk   Leopold said that almost a month later (2:3) he observed "fluent nonsense talk" for the first time. Hildegard was talking on a toy telephone and trying to impress a little boy. Later she did it for "her own entertainment (and practice!)" and did it often after that while pretending to read the newspaper. As late as 6:0, Hildegard was reported using nonsense, though at this age it was making rhymes in English and German. Her mother reported that "she often speaks nonsense in German by herself." Her father reported that he heard such soliloquies mostly in English.

As indicated by Leopold, "fluent nonsense talk" may well be interpreted as language practice at times. It may be a strategy that is used in acquiring language when other strategies have failed. This was how I interpreted Jennie's fluent nonsense talk. When it was first observed, she was using Greg as a model. Jennie stood beside him as he was talking to their mother. Jennie gave the impression she was trying to say what he was saying, repeating it about a syllable behind him. When Greg paused, she paused. When he laughed, she laughed, and when he resumed talking, she resumed her gibberish—her fluent nonsense talk. She did this repeatedly, modeling her speech after Greg, until her mother scolded her for it. It make it extremely difficult to understand Greg! Thereafter she could be heard at various times talking at this pace in her own room. No words could be discerned. At this time (2:3), Jennie was only producing one-word utterances in real speech; so the fluent nonsense talk was her first practice with sentence intonation patterns.

If my interpretation of Jennie's fluent nonsense talk is correct, her babbling was largely restricted to. what might be called purposeful babbling. She hadn't made any speech sounds as she lay in her crib, as most babies seem to do, just for the pleasure of the sound or sensation of it. Even this babbling seemed not to be for pleasure so much as for the purpose of learning to speak rapidly in the way she heard others around her speaking.

Another example of fluent nonsense talk that appears to be for the purpose of language practice is reported by Norman.[7] This girl, who was five years old, was taken by her parents to spend a holiday in France. She knew no French, while everyone else around her did, even her American friends. She learned a few words with great difficulty, but was reluctant to use them. Then Norman reports that "she hit upon a device by which she could get very much the sort of practice that she had formerly achieved through babbling, when learning her mother tongue. She began to play 'Mothers and Fathers' with another child and in this game a completely nonsensical language was talked. When asked what it was, she replied that it was rubbish—rubbish-French." She played this game repeatedly until finally her rubbish-French came to resemble true French to a "surprising degree." She was getting the proper intonation of French, and acquiring many of the sounds that occur in French but not in English. The rubbish-French helped her to dispel her embarrassment about trying to speak a language she didn't know, and she began to make good progress in learning to speak "real" French.

Parental Attitudes about Babbling   "Do not cry, my child! What are you crying for? If you wail, the leopard will devour your mother. If you wail, what befalls us is your doing! Don't cry, then, and be quiet!" This lullaby of a Chaga mother[8] speaks to the infant as though the child could understand what she is saying. Other times her words are more soothing: "Be quiet, my child, blessing from God; be quiet, my troubles, too. If you knew my troubles, little baby mine, how quiet you would be!" The Chaga mother talks to the baby, tells him her troubles. In speaking of the Chaga baby's babbling, Raum says that "these 'meaningless sounds' are powerful instruments evoking delightful experiences in the parents. With gleaming eyes, a Chaga mother bends over her child and reports its every 'word' to its father. He, too, is pleased and imagines that already it calls him 'ba-ba-ba' or 'ta-ta-ta.' '' Chaga parents boast of the linguistic accomplishments of their babies, reporting, for example, that their baby has learned to say "mbru-mbru-mbru," a word to call the goats to be fed.

This attitude seems quite similar to that of American parents who are very pleased and proud of their infants' vocalizations. Part of our "folk wisdom" seems to be that the child who speaks some words very early must surely be brighter than a child who dawdles at this task. This is not true, of course, but it often prompts parents to attribute meaning to babblings whenever they can, even though it may involve a considerable stretch of the imagination.[9]

A contrast to these attitudes may be found in other cultures. A study by Caudill and Weinstein[10] indicates that Japanese mothers do not tend to chat with their children in the way that Chaga and American mothers do. In a sample of 776 children in the Tohoku area of northern Japan studied by Arai, Ishikawa, and Toshima, and reported by Caudill and Weinstein, Japanese infants matched American norms in vocalization from ages 4 to 16 weeks, but after that there was a steady decline from the norms in the Japanese scores for both motor and language development from 4 months to 36 months of age. These authors report that language aptitude is the weakest behavior of the Japanese children, with a developmental quotient of 66.0 percent. The fact that the children fall within the normal range at the earliest ages and only later exhibit slow language development suggests that these are learned differences. The Japanese do not encourage speech production in their children in the way Americans or the Chagas do. The American mother, Caudill and Weinstein conclude, is in greater vocal interaction with her infant than the Japanese mother and stimulates him to greater physical activity and exploration, while the Japanese mother is in greater bodily contact with the infant and "soothes him toward physical quiescence and passivity with regard to his environment." The rearing of Korean children is very similar to that of the Japanese. Korean informants state that Korean children are required to be silent at the dinner table or in the presence of adults—silence is an important part of good manners. If a child is encouraged from infancy on to be silent, it may inhibit babbling and other kinds of vocal play even if the mother isn't consciously trying to silence this kind of "noise."

Jennie, and Karen, another child who is Jennie's age, are both Korean and were brought to the United States at 0:5 for adoption. Both of these girls were nonbabblers and somewhat slow in speech production.

Whether or not any of this can be attributed to having been conditioned to be quiet while they were in foster homes in Korea cannot be known, but Caudill and Weinstein indicate that the distinctive behaviors of Japanese children regarding language development are well on the way to being learned by three to four months of age.

Nonsense, Sound Play and Poetic Language

It seemed desirable to separate the use of nonsense words, sound play, and poetic language, but when I started looking at examples, nonsense words often seemed to be made up because they rhymed and poetic language and sound play seemed to involve a good deal of nonsense. Therefore, they are all being treated together here.

Of the children whose language development I have followed, Greg seemed to find the most pleasure in playing with language. He often substituted nonsense words in sentences, such as "Here's my gloogloog," as he handed over an empty glass, laughing as he did it. He was quite inventive about his nonsense words, but I have no long list of them because he seldom played in this way when the tape recorder was on. This kind of language play most often accompanied boisterous play.

Jespersen[11] points out that children "take delight in varying the sounds of real words, introducing, for instance, alliterations (repetitions of sounds) such as 'Sing a song of sixpence, A socket full of sye.' " That rhyme sounds precisely like something Greg might have said, but not any of the other five children. From 3:0 to 3:6 Greg also enjoyed making up rhymes such as this one with a substitution of the first consonant of a word by the consonant cluster *st*: "Dad, dad, stick and stad," "Horse, horse, stick and storse," etc. Jespersen says that at 3:1 his son Frans amused himself by making all words of a verse line he had learned begin with *d*, then the same words begin with *t*. Greg's and Frans' exercises were very similar (as well as John's "P language," discussed later).

Garvey[12] reports that a boy (2:10) picked up a toy dunebuggy in the nursery school he attended. An observer named the toy for him, and then left the room. The child subsequently played with the sounds of the word, changing the stress pattern from *dúnebuggỳ* to *dúne bú-gỳ*. Next he changed the initial consonant of the word from *d* to *j*, and then duplicated the sound: *juńe juńe bú-gỳ*. Finally he changed the rhythm and intonation contour as he chanted the word. She reports that throughout this three-minute sequence, the child was walking around the room looking at other things, not playing with the dunebuggy. The word—not the toy—was the fascination.

Keenan[13] recorded the speech of her twin boys, age 2:9, during the early morning hours in their bedroom. No adult was present during the recording. She found that sound play was one of the most frequently occurring types of talk between the two children. They often used a higher pitch than normally, for this play, and they accompanied it with laughter. During sound play, typically an utterance was produced, burst of laughter followed, then the utterance was repeated or modified by the other child, etc. An example follows[14] (numbers within parentheses indicated the number of times that utterance was repeated; a colon represents a lengthening of the vowel):

—/zaeki su/
—(laughing) /zæ ki su/ (2) (both laugh) /æ/ (laughing)
—/api:/
—/olp/ /olt/ /olt/
—/opi:/ (2)
—/api:/ (2) (laughing) /api/ (3)
—/ai/ /ju/
—(laughing) /ai/ /ju/ /api/ (repeats over and over) (laughs)
    /kaki/ (repeats over and over)
—/ai/ /i:/ /o:/
—/ai/ /i:/ /o/ /o:/

One of the best-known descriptions of poetic play, as well as playful language practice, is found in Weir.[15] For a period of several months, Anthony, Weir's 2½-year-old boy, talked to himself as he was getting ready to go to sleep, and she recorded these "bedtime soliloquies" by means of a voice-activated microphone hidden in his room, which was quite dark.

An example of Anthony's poetic language play is analyzed by Weir:

Like a piggy bank (repeated 2 times)   k p g b n k
Had a pink sheet on   p n k
The grey pig out   g p g

Anthony seemed to have a special fondness for the velar consonants (k, g, nk, ng) in his sound play, and he repeated these sounds again and again. In another instance he made up syllables for a rhyme:

/bink/   (bink)
/lɛt boubɔ biŋk/   (let Bobo bink)

/bɪnk bɛn bɪŋk/   (bink ben bink)
/blu kɪŋk/   (blue kink)

This rhyme contained the same velar consonants, but with nonsense words, with the exception of *let* and *Bobo*, a favorite toy of Anthony's.

Anthony was unaware of the microphone in his room. Close to 3,000 utterances were recorded during these bedtime soliloquies over a period of about two and a half months. No aspect of his utterances could be thought of as communication. In some cases he seems to be practicing language and in some cases just enjoying the sounds he was making. While no other study has included such a large sample of private speech at bedtime, or when the child was in isolation, many parents have reported that their children indulged in this kind of language play.

Britton[16] reports that Karen, who was 2:8, was staying for a week with other family members while her mother was in a hospital, and talked to herself while she was getting ready to go to sleep. Although she wasn't alone in the room, she answered her own questions and seemed not to expect anyone else to respond to her speech. The following soliloquy took place as Karen was settling down in a strange bed with her nylon rabbit, wrapped in a scarf:

Nice and soft in my bed
Nice and soft in bed.
I'm like a bunny-rabbit now
Wrapped up like a bunny-rabbit now—
I'm getting soft like a bunny-rabbit—
Yes, like a bunny-rabbit
Bunnies are soft like feathers.
Dogs are soft, too, and lambs are soft.
I like things soft, don't you?
Yes, I like things soft.

Karen was fascinated with softness here, even including herself as something that was "getting soft." Other soliloquies are more concerned with her mother's absence:

When I'm little bit older,
When I'm little bit older,
I'll have a cup of tea,
I'll have a cup of tea,
When I'm little bit older,
When Mummy comes back again.

While Karen's soliloquies have no communicative function, they don't seem to be entirely playful, either. She seems to be concerned with comforting herself until her mother comes to get her. Yet, each soliloquy has its own theme and word repetitions and qualifies as poetic language.

In contrast to the presleep soliloquies, which require no audience, Britton offers examples of what he calls "spiels" in which the child is performing, though he does not expect any audience participation. The fact of its being a performance can be indicated in several ways: it may be said in a singsong voice or sung, or it may be accompanied by rhythmical movements, perhaps resembling a dance. The following example by a child, Clare, who was almost three, was accompanied by singsong tones:[17]

> There was a little girl called May
> and she had some dollies—
> and the weeds were growing in the ground—
> and they made a little nest out of sticks
> for another little birdie up in the trees
> and they climbed up the tree—
> and the weeds were growing in the ground
>   (*I can do it much better if there's some food in my tum!*)
> The weeds were growing in the ground—
> the ghee (?) was in the sun and it was a Sunday—
> Now we all gather at the seaside
> and the ghee was in London having dinner in a dinner-shop
> and the weeds were growing in the ground—
> and we shall go there again—we shall go there again—
> we shall go there again
> 'cos it's a nice Sunday morning and a fine day
> and we had a pony
> and the weeds were growing in the ground.

Britton refers to the performance as a kind of "celebration" with fragments of past experience caught up into it. In the sentence, "I can do it much better . . ." he believes that the *it* refers to the performance. The performance is more concerned with rhythm than with individual words, or with word repetitions, such as were found in Anthony's soliloquies. Each child has his own style in poetic language, just as mature poets do.

Shorter segments of poetic and playful language were found in conversation and a story retelling task with a group of Yakima Indian children between the ages of 3:10 and 5:9. In a similar group of middle-class non-Indian children I found that the Yakima children had a much more playful attitude in general about the use of language than the non-Indian children. Sometimes words were repeated for the rhythmic, poetic effect. Here are some examples from several Yakima children:

He put him in a little boat. Little boaty boat.

And there's his mama shoes and there's mama bananas and mama peaches.

And it was George. Georgie Porgie. There goes Georgie Porgie! Georgie Porgie!

He flied up and he's real tight. There he goes, really, real tight, way up in the sky. Up in the air. (Said with greatly exaggerated intonation contours.)

Then the watcher was right down there so he won't get out, so washed and quietly. (*Watcher=watchman*, and *washed* probably means *hushed*, as it was said in a loud whisper.)

(looking at picture of trailer boats) Trailer boats, trailer boats, trailer boats. (He started with a high pitch on the first two words, medium pitch on the next repetition, and a low pitch on the last.)

And the man can . . . up up up up up up up up up. (She used a steadily rising intonation on the *up's.*)

(looking at picture of boats) There's another ship, 'nother ship, 'nother ship, 'nother ship. (in a singsong)

Some of the examples were very musical. During one conversation a little boy noticed a picture of a train, and said, "That's a choo-choo train." Then he repeated "choo-choo train" three times as though it were a song, similar to the "trailer boats" example, but it was a different boy doing it.

The Yakima children used sound effects freely, and seemed to use their nonsense words for a variety of purposes:

Nyaaaaa look at his popo. . . . Nyaaaa look at his feet. Awwww. And the water blukkkkk.

And he calleded up it and the line and ding, ding, and he said "orboo, orboo."

And then he said "det det."

And he said "gring, gring, gring."

Mik mik mik mak, mik mik mik mak. (Looking at a picture of fish.)

I believe that the great number of examples of linguistic play found in the speech of the Yakima children is due to an attitude in their culture that is related to language being used for entertainment purposes. The Yakimas, as with other native Americans, have a tradition of well-developed oral skills. Such oral skills are valued more highly in their culture than in ours.[18]

The discussion until now has centered on the child's origination of nonsense or poetic formations. Even children who don't make up nonsense freely may appreciate it. Fred, for example, only rarely made up nonsense words, but at 2:5, I read him Lewis Carroll's Jabberwocky (from *Through the Looking-Glass*). I wanted to see if he would think any of the words were funny or if he might assume they were simply words he didn't know.[19] He remained silent through the "slithy toves," and "Jubjub bird," the "frumious Bandersnatch," and all the other nonsense in the first four verses. But in the fifth verse, when I came to "snicker-snack." he repeated it after me, "Snicker snack?" and laughed out loud. Then he started commenting on each nonsese word after I had read it. "Galumphing?" he laughed. "Callooh! Callay?" By the time I finished reading it, he said, "Read that story again." This time he laughed at the words from the very beginning, and laughed almost continuously. I had given him no warning that the poem would be funny, and it had taken him a little while to decide how to react to it.

Of the children whose language development I have followed closely, Fred seemed to have acquired all aspects of language the most rapidly and easily, but he was not particularly inclined to play with language and he was never heard using any "practice routines" such as Leslie used frequently and such as Anthony Weir used.[20]

Games

In this section I have included only a few examples which seem to be representative of the kinds of games, first, that children initiate and second, that adults initiate. There is a rich literature on children's games, particularly after children reach school age, but because this topic is already so well covered, it will not be treated here. Rather, this chapter focuses on the origins and development of language games at earlier ages.

Games Initiated by the Child   Beyond the babbling period children devise countless ways to have fun with language. Some children seem to enjoy poetic sounds (such as Greg's rhyming words in the introduction to this chapter), unusual sounds, unusual formation, etc., much more than others. At an early age, Leslie, for example, was much more inclined to experiment with visual effects than with auditory effects. Her art work, sculpture, arrangements of her belongings in her room all suggest a keen sensitivity to unusual visual stimuli. By the time she was producing language more easily, however, she began to play with language in private situations, such as while taking a bath (see Chapter 1), and since she has been old enough to write, she has written a number of stories incorporating alliteration, rhyming, and word play. Furthermore, her schoolteachers have considered her to be an outstanding creative writer.

In language games, almost as much as in language play, it may be seen that there are great personality differences resulting in children's enjoyment of very different language activities.

The Naming Game: A game that has been reported by many child-language observers is what may be called the "Naming Game." This usually occurs at the time a child has just learned the names of many of the objects in his environment and wants to name them while an adult listens, although there are other varieties of the game. They appear in this order: the adult names something and asks the child to repeat it: "This is a ball, Can you say *ball*?" (Or the adult asks for names without naming the objects first.) Then children go through a period of asking adults to name things for them. Brown[21] says that Adam, Eve, and Sarah asked "What dat?" hundreds of times during the periods he referred to as Stages I and II. He said it was their most frequent question. It was also a favorite question for Fred, John, Gregory, and Brandon, but not for Leslie or Jennie.

This question can have two similar meanings: What is the nature or function of that object, or What is that object called? Leopold[22] remarked that Hildegard used practically no naming questions at all of the type "What do you call this?" Her "What's that?" questions were asking for more general kinds of information, and I wouldn't classify these questions as part of the Naming Game.

While Leslie asked very few questions of any kind, during the period of time that she was 2:9 to 3:0 she loved the third variety of the Naming Game—the variety in which the child names everything in sight for the benefit of an adult. She particularly liked to play it in her own room where almost all the objects were familiar to her. This gave her obvious pleasure, as she would triumphantly name correctly every object I could point to. In other rooms of the house or in other places, I sometimes asked her if she knew the name of something as a small test of her language development. Leslie's biggest problem was in introducing the game. Her usual way was to pull me into her room (she never introduced the game in any other room) and once I was there, she would point to something and name it. The first time or two she did this, I thought she was merely showing me new toys or furniture and I didn't help her play the game. She continued naming objects, pausing and looking at me after each item. Eventually I would take over the game and ask, "What's this?" as I pointed to objects. Sometimes I would point to something unusual, such as the ceiling. She usually recognized such questions as being different—breaking the rules of the game, so to speak—and we would both laugh when she produced the right name.

Another variation of the Naming Game that Leslie loved from about 3:6 to 4:6 was listing categories of various kinds, mostly kinds of categorizations that had been presented on Sesame Street. She enjoyed listing all the words she could think of that started with a certain letter of the alphabet, for example. At 4:1, she introduced the game this way:

> Leslie: Know what gookie karoucher (cookie monster) say one more K-word is, huh . . . kruddy. That a K-word.
> Weeks: Kruddy is another K-word?
> Fred: Karate!
> Weeks: Oh, karate!
> Leslie: A word that start with K? (This was said with a very high pitch, which marked it as a question. She had not yet mastered question transformations. She meant, "Do you know another word that starts with a K?")
> Weeks: What?
> Leslie: Can.
> Weeks: Well, that certainly is a k-sound. That's very good! (She was barely beginning to learn to read, and was making her judgments on sound, not on spelling.)

This game could go on and on with changes in the letters of the alphabet.

The Misnaming Game: The literature on child language acquisition seems to contain only sparse information about children playing the Misnaming Game. The information consists of isolated anecdotes. However, as suggested earlier, it appears that a child must be confident in his ability to name things correctly before he is ready to play at naming them incorrectly. Again, judging from experience with the children I have studied, there are great individual differences in the use of, and appreciation of, the Misnaming Game. I have no record of Fred engaging in it, although as was mentioned above, he thoroughly enjoyed nonsense words, started telling puns before he was four years old, and in general had a keen sense of humor. Greg, on the other hand, loved the

Misnaming Game. He frequently substituted one word for another as a way of starting a bantering kind of conversation, for example, "I'm putting my boats on," as he put his boots on. The listener is expected to respond with, "Oh, you're wearing boats today? Do you expect it to rain hard?" or something of a jocular nature. Greg started this kind of language play before he was 3:0 and continues it to the time of this writing.

In spite of the fact that Greg plays this game constantly, Jennie does not accept it as humor. When he was 5:3 and she was 2:11, Greg called their cat a giraffe, and Jennie said very earnestly to him, "No, Greg. Cat. *Our* cat." On the other hand, Jennie seemed to recognize nonsense words as humor when Greg played with them. It wouldn't seem that a child who was not yet three would necessarily know a nonsense word from an unfamiliar "real" word, but as was pointed out above, at 2:5, Fred could tell the difference. Furthermore, when Greg produced a nonsense word, he usually paused and pronounced it more slowly than a normal word, giving the impression that he was formulating the word as he spoke. This hesitation may have given Jennie a clue, if she needed one, that this word was nonsense.

The Reading Game: Almost every child who is read to tries the Reading Game sooner or later. The Reading Game consists simply of the child pretending he is reading (as in the example of Greg pretending to read in the introduction to this chapter). Sometimes this includes a very good imitation of intonation contours, and sometimes as with the case of Jennie, simply a different intonation pattern from her normal one.

Leopold reported that Hildegard didn't hear loud reading very often and was past 2:2 when she first pretended to read. She had enjoyed books before that time, but had not given her reading any vocal expression. Hildegard used the same kind of nonsense syllables for her reading that she used in singing.

Between the ages of 1:6 and 2:0, the girl whose speech development Norman[23] followed developed intonation patterns that "reached a high degree of perfection." The girl used these intonation patterns with her babbling for "reading." These sentences without words were reported to have sounded more like real speech than the child's meaningful utterances, as is the usual case.

The seven children whose language development I follow were all introduced to books at early ages, and all developed their own "reading" style, but at somewhat different ages. At 0:9 Brandon (as well as John and Fred) began to look at picture books and babble with English intonation patterns without recognizable words. Brandon's "sentences" were short, but he continued to chatter as long as he looked at the book and turned the pages. To date, Brandon has followed this pattern with every book he looks at except a Donald Duck picture book that his mother gave him when he was 1:0. He immediately recognized Donald as being a duck, pointed and said /dʌ/, as he looked at each page. He said /dʌ/ just once for each page (there was only one Donald Duck per page), and he did not include any other babbling.

For a period of several months, from 1:3 to 1:9, Jennie used a steady repetition of "dubba dubba dubba" when she was pretending to read. At 1:9 she began using a midvowel (a) when she pretended to read. With either of these two "reading" sounds, she varied the pitch so that it was more like singing than like a good imitation of sentence intonation patterns.

A second kind of "reading" involved some understandable English words along with babbling. Leslie began doing this at 1:6. As she turned the pages of picture books, it was possible to follow her scanning of the pictures, because she threw in names of things she saw, but filled in her "sentences" with sounds that could not be translated. It was simple to determine the ends of her "sentences" because there was a clear falling tone and a pause. When she read stories, as described below, she gave the definite impression of knowing exactly what she was saying. Whether or not some of it may have been babbling mixed up with meaningful words cannot be stated with certainty. However, in listening and relistening to the tapes and looking at the books she was "reading," words that sounded like babbling on the first transcription suddenly took on meaning as I discovered something in the picture I hadn't noticed before. The vowels that were interspersed throughout her reading were also in all her conversation and seemed to operate as function words, or place holders, for her.

The following Reading Game session took place when Leslie was 2:11.

Leslie: /thæ boy e gʌmbi bʌth. i kie ʌ i wi   wʌn bʌth
   (that boy   bus.   he real one bus.)
   æ ŋ i dɪr   i nau i kæ we . . . i . . . boy i gu
   (dinner now can   boy)
   gʌh i bubagʰ bukth/
   (box box)
Weeks: Box?
Leslie: /bak bak bakʃ e maɪk ku maɪ wrʃ maɪ we/
   (box box box   my my way)

This constitutes about one-tenth of this story-reading session. I always have the feeling that if I were to spend enough time on the transcription, I might be able to translate more of it, but the percentage of her normal conversation that can't be understood is about the same as this sample. Because of Leslie's great difficulty with the sound system of the language, I never assumed that the fact that neither her family nor I could understand a word meant that it wasn't a meaningful word for her—I did not automatically relegate it to babbling, as is sometimes done.

The third phase is "reading" printed matter (rather than just looking at pictures) and using words that have meaning but which, of course, are not the words that are printed. An example of this took place when Jennie was 2:11 and she went with her parents to the Department of Motor Vehicles where her father was renewing his driver's license. Jennie sat with her mother on a bench, and an old man sat down beside her. Jennie had a form, containing both printed words and blanks, Jennie held it up and showed it to the man. He asked, "Do you know what this says?" She said she didn't.[24] He pretended to read, "I'm a good girl." Jennie studied the paper, and the man left soon. Several minutes later, a woman sat down and Jennie said, "Paper." The woman asked her what she was going to do with it, and Jennie answered, "I don't know. Read." The woman took the paper and said, "It says, I am a very pretty little girl. I am a good girl." Again, Jennie took the paper and looked at it. After they were both gone, Jennie's mother began to wonder, as Jennie continued to study the form, if she realized that the two adults, who were not together and had not heard each other, were playing a game with her, or if she really believed that those words were written on the paper. So her mother asked, "Can you read the paper to me, Jennie?" Jennie followed the words on the paper with her finger as she read in her usual conversational manner, with short pauses between each word, "Mom and Dad wikes me!"

Perhaps each reader will have his own interpretation of Jennie's "reading," but it does seem to illustrate that she figured out that the printed page represented words, and that she was as capable as anyone of saying what the words were.

Jennie should not be considered a usual example of the acquisition of imitation-reading skills because children are already in the process of acquiring intonation patterns of the language they hear by 0:5—the month in which Jennie was brought to the United States. It is even possible that her singsong reading tones may represent a mixture of Korean and English intonation. It may also be that children associate story reading by an adult with something quite different from conversation, or other kinds of speaking, because of the peculiarities of the storytelling register (a style of speaking that changes according to use), which is ordinarily used in this activity. This register includes a greater range in pitch and volume, more lengthening of vowels, and other expressive features of voice production than in other kinds of speaking. Jennie, for example, did not use her singsong pattern at any other time. The fact that Hildegard used the same kind of nonsense syllables for her reading that she used in singing may also be an indication that children associate story reading with singing, perhaps more than conversation, for example.

To sum up "reading," it seems to be that:

1. Children who have been read aloud to go through a stage first when they use speech sounds along with sentence intonation patterns that are too advanced for any meaningful sentences they could possibly produce. If the adult story reader uses a conversational register in reading the story, the child will probably be using sentence intonations that are simply too advanced for sentences he will be producing himself for perhaps two or three years. If, on the other hand, the adult reader uses storytelling register features consistently, the child may be acquiring intonation patterns that he probably will never use again except in storytelling activities, that is, patterns that are more exaggerated than are usually used in conversation.

2. A second stage that some children go through includes these same patterns, but with some real words thrown in. At this stage, what the child says is still judged meaningless by adults, though it may be the case that children have an intended meaning that is not expressed understandably for the adult.

3. A third stage is represented by simpler intonation patterns, and real meaning on the part of the child, even though his "reading" is still an imitation, simply because the child has not yet learned to read. The reading material may be either printed matter or pictures, or both.

Repeating Nursery Rhymes: Opie and Opie[25] point out that nursery rhymes are propagated not by children but by adults. They are rhymes that are approved by adults and taught to children by adults, and are therefore categorized here as games, rather than as play (which is more unstructured and created by children).

Nursery rhymes have a universal appeal, perhaps because of the rhythm. Burling[26] offers some examples of Chinese, Benkulu, and English rhymes. They all follow similar themes and have similar rhythms. The patterns found in children's rhymes are not limited to that area, of course. They are found in adult rhymes, also.

Two of the earliest rhymes that are taught to babies are Pat-a-Cake and This Little Pig Goes to Market. Both involve play that the child enjoys. There are many variations of both. In Pat-a-Cake, or Patty Cake, the words and actions follow:

> Patty cake, patty cake, Baker's man (Adult helps the child clap hands)
> Bake a little cake as fast as you can (Clapping increases in speed)
> Roll it and pat it and toss it up high (Child's hands are rolled over each other)
> And put it in the oven for baby and I. (Child's hands are pulled up as high as they will go)

Some parents have modified the last line to make it grammatically "correct."

Aside from simply enjoying the attention, babies usually enjoy the physical aspects of the game, and often learn to ask for the game in some way. One of Leslie's first five monoremes (one-word utterances) was /bæ bæ/, presumably for "pat, pat" and it meant she wanted to play Patty Cake. Likewise, the physical play in This Little Pig is enjoyable to most children. The adult touches or moves the baby's toes as he repeats the rhyme. Again, *piggy* is a frequently found word in children's early vocabularies. It was among the first 50 words for both Jennie and Leslie.

Many examples can be found of children repeating nursery rhymes but changing the words slightly so that they have meaning for the child, but the rhythm is usually maintained. Leopold, however, reported that Hildegard's mother had read the story of the three little kittens who lost their mittens to Hildegard when she was 2:1. In Hildegard's version of it, all the rhythm was lost, and some words of the original rhyme had been replaced by Hildegard's own synonyms:

/wi mi au jɔʃ mɪti/	Three meows lost mittens
/ʔo memi dia/	Oh mammy dear!
/ʒu nɔi mi au/	You naughty meows.
/ʔɔ: pu/	All pooh
/no paɪ/	No pie.

Meow was Hildegard's word for kitten, and *pooh* was her word for soiled. This was obviously not an attempt at imitation, but was her own recreation of the story.

Leopold[27] remarked that Hildegard had no appreciation of rhyme, but a marked sense of rhythm.

At 4:8 Hildegard made up her first rhyme:

> Einmal da war ein Voglein auf die Baume,
> Vater war schutteling die Flaume.

Kornei Chukovsky, the Russian poet and keen observer of children, offers many insights into children's language play. In discussing the purpose of play, he says,[28] "It is not humor that the child seeks when he plays this kind of game; his main purpose, as in all play, is to exercise his newly acquired skill of verifying his knowledge of things. We know that the child—and this is the main point—is amused by the reverse juxtaposition of things only when the real juxtaposition has become completely obvious to him. No sooner, for instance, does he acquaint himself with the most useful truth, that heat burns, than he is ready to derive great fun from the jolly English folk song about a droll person who burned himself with cold porridge. . . . When we notice that a child has started to play with some newly acquired component of understanding, we may definitely conclude that he has become full master of this item of understanding; only those ideas can become toys for him whose proper relation to reality is firmly known to him."

Chukovsky points out that rural Russian children are familiar with horses as being animals that one rides, but that their folk verses are invariably nonsensical in alluding to riding all manner of animals except horses:

> And old woman mounted a sheep
> And rode up the mountain steep . . .
>
> Get on a terrier
> Ride to the Farrier . . .
>
> Masha left her hut so narrow
> To take a ride on a tiny sparrow . . .

He adds, "Children make every effort to substitute for the horse any kind of nonsensical alternate, and the more palpable the nonsense the more enthusiastically does the children's rhyme cultivate it:

> The cook rode on a rickety van
> Harnessed to a frying pan.

Nonsense is an essential element of nursery rhymes. The child is aware of what is usual and normal but wants to exercise his imagination with what is not normal. Animals talk, people ride on sparrows, cows jump over the moon, and fairies and giants abound. The impossible is the usual in the world of nursery rhymes.

Pig Latins: One of the most sophisticated types of linguistic play or game involves reordering, substituting, adding segments, etc., to language. In some cultures this is indulged in freely by adults, and in other cultures, such as ours, it is principally used by older children. Pig Latin is such a game. It is not always easy to determine when a linguistic activity should be labeled a game or play, but there are rules involved in the use of pig latins which qualify them as games. However, a child's participation at any given time depends on peer groups; one ordinarily does not play it alone.

The rule in pig latin is that the initial consonant or consonant cluster of a word is moved from the first of the word to the last of the word, and the vowel *a* is added at the end: pig latin→igpey atinley. Children often use it or other such codes as a "secret" language. Since most adults also learned to use it during early school years, probably the only persons who don't understand it would be younger children. In this case, the purpose of pig latin may be more related to establishing group boundaries than to finding pleasure in language.

Children throughout the world use such phonological devices to create secret languages. A number of examples are given by Burling.[29] One example he gives is that of Arabic speakers in Cairo. The children here insert *tin* plus a vowel before the final syllable of each polysyllabic word, but the second vowel of the insertion echoes the preceding normal vowel:

/huwa ha jedihali/ ("He will give-it-me.")
/hutinuwa ha jedihatinali/

The variations with such pig latins are endless.

Among the Hanunoo in the Philippines, Conklin[30] reported several ways of changing the language for linguistic play. The overall manner of articulation or vocalization of a sentence may be altered by: (1) whispering; (2) using clipped pronunciation, typified by greater speed, greater tension of the throat muscles, expansion of intonational contours (greater range in pitch), and shortening of long vowels; (3) using a falsetto (an artifically high voice); (4) changing the flow of air, that is, producing air flow entirely by inhalation instead of exhalation. In addition to these techniques, they may substitute vowels or consonants, or they may say the opposite of what they mean; that is, they may say that something is very bad when they mean it is very good. Since there are no semantically opposite forms for many lexical items or expressions, this last technique is necessarily limited. In this case, these linguistic changes are made principally for courting behavior, but not exclusively so. Males of courting age are also expected to master the "art of facile, rapid conversation, in which the highest value is placed on the most indirect method of statement."

In a paper that analyzed the principles by which children construct secret languages, and to what extent the properties of such principles are matched by or deviate from properties or principles found in ordinary languages, Guile and Suzman[31] found that the rules that children avail themselves of require very little in the way of grammatical information, just word and stem boundaries and some category information. Ordinarily, transposed segments occur within a word (that is, *"get* lost" becomes "et*g*ay ostlay," not "etay ost*g*lay"). Also, operations introducing segments are usually vowel-oriented rather than consonant-oriented in that material introduced is inevitably introduced adjacent to a vowel rather than adjacent to a consonant. That is, a vowel must be mentioned in the structural description of the rules. Also, segments are generally introduced in such a way that the results are sequences of the consonant-vowel type. Words or morphemes are usually not rearranged.

Related to pig latins, in that sounds are substituted in a rule-ordered way, is a "counting language" that John used at 6:0. He asked if I wanted him to count in "Q language, K language, or C language." I immediately chose Q language, thinking that it sounded a little tricky. After a moment's hesitation, he said, "How about P language?" He said he would count to 20, and proceeded, "Pun, poo, pee, pour, pive, pix, peven, peight, pine, pen," etc., to 20. Where there was no consonant, he inserted one. Where there was either a consonant or a consonant cluster (as with *thr*ee), he substituted a *p* for the initial sound. When he finished, I asked him where he had learned to do that kind of counting, and he said he had made it up.

As may be concluded from this description, some of these secret language games can be devised and used by children, and others, such as Conklin describes, are more complicated and beyond the capabilities of most children.

Games Initiated by Adults   The Cough Game: Among the earliest games originated by adults are those that adults often credit the infant with originating. One of these is what Call[32] refers to as the "cough game." It begins when the baby coughs and the mother imitates the baby and smiles. The baby may not cough again immediately, but if the mother plays this little game again, the baby will sooner or later cough in return, and the game is in full swing. The mother and baby take turns coughing and laughing. Later the baby may initiate the game himself, and the mother may be convinced that the baby invented the game.

Call points out that for the mother the Cough Game, which he has observed as early as two months, is one of the first forms of positive communication with the baby, even though it is not verbal communication. For the baby it is a sign of his own power to control the world.

It should be emphasized that a cough, for example, is not likely to strike the baby as being something amusing in itself. It is the mother's playful attitude toward the cough that creates a game out of it. Therefore, we may see that from the very earliest ages parental attitudes will shape the child's sense of humor—his attitude toward a playful approach to his environment.

Other aspects of mother-infant interaction are discussed in Chapter 2.

Peekaboo: One of the earliest games with what may be thought of as a consistent structure is peekaboo. While the game varies with different persons and with the age of the child, it is definitely rule-ordered. Bruner and Sherwood[33] observed six infants over a period of ten months, from seven to seventeen months of age, and their mothers. The mother-child pair were observed every other week for an hour and the mother was asked to play the games her infant enjoyed most. Peekaboo was one of the favorites, and an analysis of the videotapes made of the mother-infant pairs indicated that the basic rules of peekaboo are: initial contact, disappearance, reappearance, and reestablished contact. Bruner and Sherwood[34] add, "Within this rule context, there can be variations in degree and kind of vocalization for initial contact, in kind of mask, in who controls the mask, in whose face is masked, in who uncovers, in the form of vocalization upon uncovering, in the relation between uncovering and vocalization, and in the timing of the constituent elements (though this last is strikingly constrained by a capacity variable). What the child appears to be learning is not only the basic rules of the game, but the range of variation that is possible within the rule set. It is this emphasis upon patterned variation within a constraining rule set that seems crucial to the mastery of competence and generativeness."

The laboratory setting of this experiment limited the possible variations somewhat in that the baby's blanket seemed to be the only way of hiding the face. By the time Kara was 0:10, she loved playing peekaboo with me when I hid behind another person. It was not easy to get acquainted with Kara even after several visits, as she was very wary of strangers; so I tried peekaboo first with her while she was secure in her mother's arms. I ducked down behind her mother, out of Kara's sight, and then reappeared over her mother's shoulder. I got my first smile from Kara for my efforts. A month later, Kara was standing beside a chair, Brandon (1:9) was standing beside her, but facing me, and I was sitting on the floor. I hid my head behind Brandon, then peeked around him and said "Boo!" Kara laughed out loud, and she and I became good friends. Brandon stood as still as a statue, watching the procedure, and smiled rather condescendingly, I thought, at the childish procedure. Not that 1:9 is too old for peekaboo, but it is only entertaining to the child who is being surprised. As late as age five, Fred, John, Leslie, Greg, and Jennie all enjoyed an occasional peekaboo-type surprise if they happened to be in the bedroom when I was making the bed, and a sheet that I was trying to put on the bed just happened to engulf them, hiding them entirely. Making the bed could easily take as much as 20 minutes with a small child in the room!

The importance of this game in its initial stages lies not in the fact that the infant is learning to say "boo!" but in the fact that the child is learning to integrate a surprisingly wide range of phenomena into rule structures, much as he integrates the language he hears into a rule-structured system. No one explains the rules of the game to the child, just as no one explains the rules of grammar to the child; he must deduce the rules for himself. And he does.

Who You For?: Games in which an adult asks a question or makes a remark that requires a certain response by the child vary with the culture but are common throughout the world. In a black community on the Mississippi River near New Orleans, for example, mothers teach their babies to take part in this little game as soon as they learn to talk:[35]

> Mother: Who you for, chere?
> Child: You.
> Mother: (laughs) Who that? Who you for, chere?
> Child: Rosa.
> Mother: Rosa who?
> Child: Rosa Abadie.

The child is not supposed to say "you" or "mama" but is supposed to answer with the proper name of its mother. The mother laughs at the wrong answer and repeats the game until the child answers with her full proper name. The child is always rewarded by a hug or a kiss.

Such games, wherever they are found, are used not only to amuse but to inspire tenderness and affection.

The Misnaming Game as Initiated by Adults: Why is it that some children find many things amusing and other children live in a very serious world? How will the child react to attempts at humor if introduced by strangers? Will he be puzzled or amused?

Davison[36] reports on an experiment she tried with two French-speaking children, Jean and Sophie. Jean was 2:2 and Sophie was 3:4. Another child whom she intended to include in her experiment had to be eliminated because he didn't recognize the kind of nonserious speech events that she was introducing, nor did he engage in them. Davison suggests that linguistic play results when certain conventions of language use are broken intentionally. In the section on language play originated by children, some examples of this were given, such as Greg calling their cat a *giraffe* and Jennie refusing to accept this as play. Intentional misnaming can result in linguistic play only after a child is fully confident about names in his world. It may take different children different lengths of time to reach this stage of confidence.

Davison was a stranger to the children with whom she was working. Sophie had been looking at a picture book in a "question/answer period." She was looking at a picture of a basket with a dog in it and Davison asked, "C'est une table, ça?" (Is this a table?) Sophie was puzzled and turned to her mother, "Maman, c'est une table, ça?" (Mommy, is this a table?) Previous to this, Sophie had been naming objects as they were pointed out to her in the book, and it may be assumed that she knew what dogs, baskets, and tables were. Davison says that she used a "playful tone" but she doesn't mention whether or not she was facing Sophie and whether or not she smiled or gave any other clear, nonverbal indication that she was playing. Davison suggests that Sophie was following the target language assumption that "a strange speaker will avoid misleading the hearer." I assume, too, that Davison was not trying to mislead the hearer but that she was trying to break a linguistic rule (misname an object) as a means of instigating linguistic play, and that she assumed her "playful tone" would give the child the cue that she was joking. However, in order to avoid misleading the hearer, the speaker must give unmistakable cues to joking behavior, and what is unmistakable to one person may not be to another, unfortunately. We see this in adult conversation frequently. Some adults use a completely serious manner to tell a joke, and among the audience, some will never catch on to the joke—will take the story seriously—because they were looking for facial expressions or paralinguistic features (such as unusual pitch, volume, or lengthening of vowels) for cues.

In another instance, Jean initiates some language play and Sophie enters into the game. Sophie and Jean were looking at a picture of a duck in a book. Davison asked, "C'est quoi ça?" (What's this?) Sophie answered, "C'est comme on l'a vu." (It's like we saw.) Jean interposed, "Ba . . . ba ça." (Ba this.) Then he pointed to the duck. Davison replied, "C'est un canard ça." (It's a duck.) Jean insisted, "Non . . . ba." Davison asked, "Ba? Qu'est-ce que c'est que ba?" (Ba? What is ba?) This time Sophie got into the game and answered "Ça c'est du ba." (This is ba.) Davison said, "Ça c'est du ba? C'est un canard ça." (This is ba? This is a duck). Sophie insisted, "Du ba, c'est du ba." Sophie and Jean both giggled. We can see in this instance that Sophie is able to go along with the Misnaming Game. However, in this case, the wrong name was a nonsense word. The evidence offered in the Davison paper does not tell us precisely what cues Sophie used to detect the game in the case of Jean's game, and what cues she may have missed in the case of Davison's. Different rules apply, of course, when children are talking to each other than when strange adults are talking to children.

I have played the Misnaming Game at one time or another with all the children I have been working with, and almost without exception, if I initiate the game, the child quickly looks at my face for cues that I am intending it to be humorous before he answers. The cues in my voice alone do not seem to be sufficient. Davison points out the "inferential opportunities seem to develop best in fully understood circumstances; that is, the situation in which linguistic play occurs must be familiar to the child, otherwise an attempt at playful speech will go unrecognized."

I must also add that the Misnaming Game may not be one that is readily recognized as such by many children, unless it involves nonsense. Even conditioning at home, such as Jennie had from Greg, may not be enough to help a child recognize misnaming as being humorous. Nonsense games would appear to be more popular and more easily recognized as game-playing than misnaming.

Nelson[37] conducted an experiment with 16 children over a period of a year. At age 20 to 21 months, she had the mother of each child show the child colored pictures of objects and read a sentence referring to the picture, for example, "See it's a _____ . Can you say _____?" In some cases the object was correctly named and sometimes incorrectly named. Nelson reports,[38] "Surprisingly, the number of imitations was no different for pictures that did *not* match the object word than for those that did (mean scores of 1.7 and 1.8 respectively)." While Nelson refers to this as a "game," she does not report any puzzlement or amusement on the part of the children, even when the correct name was in their productive vocabulary and their mother was calling it by another name. I would speculate that early age and the fact that it was their own mother who was asking them to repeat the wrong name made a difference in their accepting behavior.

Discussion

Play is an activity that has no purpose other than amusement or pleasure. Likewise, language play does not serve to communicate but to amuse. In a paper that attempts to explain play, Reilley[39] says, "Play behavior that occurs early in childhood, or play behavior that occurs when an event is very new or different, is characterized by exploration. It is engaged in for its own sake, and fulfills in all ways the requirement for intrinsic motivation." Play must be free from the sense of compulsion or external restraint. Reilly also suggests that play activity takes place only when major needs are in abeyance. The child cannot indulge in exploratory play when he is in a state of anxiety or great physical or emotional need. If a child reaches a point where he never wants to play, a parent is correct in assuming that he is in need of professional attention.

Cazden[40] discusses the essential nature of play in the developmental process and cites Mattick[41] as evidence that the absence of play with language has a negative effect. Mattick studied children of "disorganized lower-class families" and specifically mentions that "there was a lack of exploration of language and an absence of the usual play with words which facilitates increasing communicative skills and serves to extend knowledge!"[42]

The importance of play in the development of children has been recognized for many years. For some children language play has an important role in helping them to express feelings that are not easily expressed in other ways and to demonstrate their individuality. It may play an important role in the acquisition of both the first and the second language.

Developmental Order   As was suggested above, children do not seem to play with aspects of language before they feel confident in their use of that aspect. A study by Sanches and Kirshenblatt-Gimblett[43] may offer some evidence on this point, though with older children. They collected rhymes and various kinds of speech play from a total of 301 children ranging in age from five to fourteen. They suggest for young children the phonological component (sounds) of language is much more strongly organized than the syntactic (sentence structure), semantic (meaning), or sociolinguistic (appropriate usage), and this seems also to be the case with the children I observe. Sanches and Kirshenblatt-Gimblett also suggest that there is a developmental order (beyond phonological) in the kinds of language play that children indulge in: there is a shift from phonological to grammatical to semantic, and finally to the sociolinguistic level of language, and that aspects of language are played with in the order in which they are mastered. Cazden challenges this order, in part because language is not learned by levels. Cazden argues,[44] "Sounds seem to be learned first because children's vocalizations are identified as speech only when they conform to recognized sound patterns, but, in fact, meanings begin to be acquired before any words are spoken and continue to be acquired throughout life." From the adult point of view, children play with sounds first because that is what they are producing first. If we think of syntax as consisting not only of the order of words or morphemes in an utterance, but of the sentence intonation pattern as well, it may be seen that many children are using such patterns in a playful way by the time they are five months old or so. By this time many children hold "prespeech conversations" with adults in which the babbling sounds are similar to language without meaningful words. This may reasonably be thought of as language play with the paralinguistic features, at least, of syntax (the rising and falling patterns of sentences).

Perhaps all we can say for certain about the developmental order in the acquisition of language play is that children must have a minimal control over an aspect of language before they can play with it. Children cannot play with words before they produce words or experiment with stress patterns in sentences before they are producing sentences (that is, two-word utterances as a minimum). More research and observation is needed in this area.

Summary

Observers of child language in many cultures have reported that children engage in language play and games. This activity may be assumed to be universal, though there are great individual differences in the extent to which language is played with and enjoyed. Language play is engaged in for its own sake; it does not of necessity fulfill any other language function. The function of language play is to provide pleasure.

Children do not begin to play with aspects of language that they have not "mastered" (to use Chukovsky's term). Children who are in a state of anxiety or emotional need do not indulge in language play. Given the proper conditions (emotional and physical well-being, motivation, etc.), any aspect of language—sounds, words, sentence structure, meaning, sociolinguistic rules, or paralinguistic features—may be altered for a playful effect.

Babbling, the earliest form of language play to develop, is something that children universally engage in at one age or another and find pleasure in. While Leopold says that "all observers of child language report" linguistic games with nonsense syllables, the age at which different children engage in such games varies greatly and the intensity with which children enjoy such games also varies greatly. Up to age three or so, some children may respond to conversational attempts more readily with appropriate nonverbal response, such as smiling and laughter, instead of babbling or attempted speech. Either babbling or smiling and laughter may be employed as a social response or as a private pleasure, such as when a child is alone in his crib or at play. Fluent nonsense talk, a variety of babbling, may be interpreted as language practice in the case of some children.

Some cultural differences in language play include: Cultures such as that of the Chaga speakers of Africa and the mainstream of American culture place an importance on wordlike babblings of babies and take great pleasure in the children's babblings, while in other cultures, such as the Japanese and Korean, parents prefer happy, quieter babies and do not read anything of importance into early babbling sounds. Also, preschool Yakima Indian children were found to engage more in language play—to use more nonsense words, repetitions, and poetic effects in conversation and story retelling—than non-Indian children of the same age. From the very earliest ages, parental attitudes shape the child's attitudes toward a playful approach to language and to his environment.

Examples of some of the ways children play with language are shown in Figure 2.

Children are universally reported to enjoy nonsense in language and to accept it as play. Naming things (the Naming Game) and pretending to read (the Reading Game) are two more linguistic activities that children usually enjoy.

Games such as the Misnaming Game in which an object is given the name of another real object may not be readily recognized as play by many children. Introducing a nonsense word instead of a "real" word makes it a better candidate for a "game." Nursery rhymes are propagated by adults, not children, and the repetition of such by children cannot be categorized with the invention of rhymes, nonsense words, or other ways of changing the language by children themselves for a playful effect. Older children enjoy more sophisticated linguistic games, such as pig latin, and often invent such codes, perhaps as a means of having a "secret" way of communicating with peers.

Figure 2   Examples of language play engaged in by children from ages of about 0:2 to 5:0, including sound play, nonsense words, rhyming, poetry, alliteration, similes, puns, and the Misnaming Game.

It may be concluded, then, not only that language play offers pleasure to the child who indulges in it, but also that a certain amount of play and exploration with language may be essential for the child's linguistic and cognitive development and may be a vital factor in second language acquisition as well. While parental attitudes may stifle or encourage the development of language play, a lack of language playfulness does not necessarily indicate that such activity has been discouraged. It may simply indicate a personality trait; children such as Jennie and Leslie are happy and playful, but not with language. Children use language in very different ways.

NOTES

1. Lewis, M. M. *Language, Thought and Personality*, New York: Basic Books, 1963, p. 20.

2. Lenneberg, Eric H. *Biological Foundations of Language*, New York: Wiley, 1967.

3. Jakobson, Roman. *Child Language Aphasia and Phonological Universals*, The Hague: Mouton, 1968.

4. For example, Oller, D. K., Leslie A. Wieman, William J. Doyle, and Carol Ross. "Child Speech, Babbling and Phonological Universals," in *Papers and Reports in Child Language Development*, April 1974, 33-41, and Gilbert, John H. "On Babbling: Some Physiological Observations," in *Papers and Reports on Child Language Development*, April 1974, 42-49.

5. Norman, E. "Some Psychological Features of Babble," in *Proceedings of the 2nd International Congress of Phonological Sciences*, edited by Daniel Jones and D. B. Fry, London: Cambridge University Press, 1936.

6. Leopold, Werner F. *Speech Development of a Bilingual Child*, vol. II, Evanston, Ill.: Northwestern University Press, 1949, p. 11.

7. *Op. cit.*

8. Chaga is a Bantu language of Africa. See Raum, O. F. *Chaga Childhood*, London: Oxford University Press, 1940.

9. Earlier language development may, however, indicate that a child is more skilled verbally than the one who is slower at language development. In the mainstream American culture, verbal skills are often equated with intelligence, while nonverbal skills are underrated. These attitudes vary in different cultures. To oversimplify the situation, it might be said that in some cultures the person who can do things is rated more highly than the person who can talk about things, but not in our culture. In my data, Fred and Leslie offer a good example of contrasting skills. Their IQs are comparable, but Fred is more articulate than Leslie.

10. Caudill, William, and Helen Weinstein. "Maternal Care and Infant Behavior in Japan and America," in *Reading in Child Behavior and Development*, edited by Celia Stendler Lavatelli and Faith Stendler, New York: Harcourt Brace Jovanovich, 1974.

11. Jespersen, Otto. *Language: Its Nature, Development and Origin*, New York: W. W. Norton, 1922, p. 149.

12. Garvey, Catherine. *Play*, Cambridge, Mass.: Harvard University Press, 1977, p. 63.

13. Keenan, Elinor O. "Conversational Competence in Children," *Journal of Child Language*, 1974, 1:163-183.

14. *Ibid.*, p. 171.

15. Weir, Ruth Hirsch. *Language in the Crib*, The Hague: Mouton, 1962.

16. Britton, James. *Language and Learning*, Middlesex, England: Penguin Books, 1970.

17. *Ibid.*, p. 84.

18. Lewis, Michael, and Peggy Ban ("Variance and Invariance in the Mother-Infant Interaction: A Cross-Cultural Study," paper presented at the Burg Wartenstein Symposium, Cultural and Social Influences in Infancy and Childhood, Burg Wartenstein, Austria, June 18-26, 1973) have stressed the need to consider differing ideologies in cross-cultural studies rather than just looking at differences in behavior. They point out that "ideologies lead to certain maternal behaviors which in turn have consequences in the development of the child; however, there may be less connection between behavior and outcome than between ideology and outcome." P. 6.

19. When Fred was 6:6 he read Jabberwocky aloud to me, and when he finished I asked him, "Can you tell me, are all the words in this poem regular English words?" "No," he answered, "'twas isn't a regular English word." Soon after that, I

read Jabberwocky to John, who was 4:9, and his answer to the same question was, "Well, they're English words I don't know."

20. While Anthony's practice routines may have sounded like second-language learning practice, I suspect he was principally playing with language, while Leslie seemed to be working earnestly to learn language.

21. Brown, Roger. "The Development of *wh* Questions in Child Speech," *Journal of Verbal Learning and Verbal Behavior*, 1968, 7:279-290.

22. *Speech Development of a Bilingual Child*, vol. II, p. 68.

23. "Some Psychological Features of Babble."

24. Kornei Chukovsky (*From Two to Five*, translated and edited by Miriam Morton, Berkeley, Calif.: University of California Press, 1968) tells the story of a two-year-old boy who went for a walk with his aunt and stopped at a bookstall. "The vendor asked him,

'Can you read?'

'Yes, I can.'

He gave him a book and invited him to read. Imitating his aunt, the boy felt in his pocket and said:

'I forgot my glasses at home.' "

25. Opie, Iona, and Peter Opie. *The Lore and Language of Schoolchildren*, Oxford: Clarendon Press, 1959.

26. Burling, Robbins. *Man's Many Voices: Language in Its Cultural Context*, New York: Holt, Rinehart and Winston, 1970.

27. *Speech Development of a Bilingual Child*, vol. III, p. 68.

28. *From Two to Five*, pp. 91-103.

29. *Op. cit.*

30. Conklin, Harold C. "Linguistic Play in Its Cultural Context," in *Language in Culture and Society*, edited by Dell Hymes, New York: Harper & Row, 1964.

31. Guile, Tim, and Susan Suzman. "Some Principles of Children's Secret Languages," undated mimeographed paper, Department of Phonetics and Linguistics, University of Witwatersland, Johannesburg, South Africa.

32. Call, Justin D. "Games Babies Play," *Psychology Today*, 1970, 3 (8):34-37.

33. Bruner, Jerome S., and V. Sherwood. "Peekaboo and the Learning of Rule Structures," in *Play—Its Role in Development and Evolution*, edited by Jerome S. Bruner, Alison Jolly, and Kathy Sylva, New York: Basic Books, 1976.

34. *Ibid.*, p. 283.

35. Ward, Martha Coonfield. *Them Children: A Study of Language Learning*, New York: Holt, Rinehart and Winston, 1971.

36. Davison, Anni. "Linguistics Play and Language Acquisition," in *Papers and Reports on Child Language Acquisition*, April 1974, 179-187.

37. Nelson, Katherine. "Structure and Strategy in Learning to Talk," *Monographs of the Society for Research in Child Development*, 1973, 38, Nos. 1, 2.

38. *Ibid.*, p. 50.

39. Reilly, Mary (ed.). *Play as Exploratory Learning*, Beverly Hills: Sage Publications, 1974.

40. Cazden, Courtney B. "Play with Language and Metalinguistic Awareness: One Dimension of Language Experience," in *Dimensions of Language*, edited by Charlotte Winsor, New York: Agathon Press, Inc., 1975.

41. Mattick, Ilse. "Description of the Children," in *The Drifters: Children of Disorganized Lower-Class Families*, edited by E. Pavenstedt, Boston: Little Brown, 1967.

42. Lily Wong Fillmore ("The Role of Playfulness in Second Language Learning," paper presented at the Child Language Seminar, Stanford University, April 27, 1977) has observed Spanish-speaking children, ages 5:6 to 7:6, learning English in Berkeley, Calif., and notes that "playfulness" with language was an important factor in determining the ease with which children acquired the second language.

43. Sanches, Mary, and Barbara Kirshenblatt-Gimblett. "Children's Traditional Speech Play and Child Language." In *Speech Play: Research and Resources for Studying Linguistic Creativity*, edited by Barbara Kirshenblatt-Gimblett, Philadelphia: University of Pennsylvania Press, 1976.

44. Cazden, Courtney B. Review of *Speech Play*, edited by Barbara Kirshenblatt-Gimblett, *Harvard Educational Review*, 1977, 47:430-435, p. 431.

SUGGESTED READINGS

Bruner, Jerome S., Alison Jolly, and Kathy Sylva (eds.). *Play—Its Role in Development and Evolution*, New York: Basic Books, 1976.

Chukovsky, Kornei. *From Two to Five*, translated and edited by Miriam Morton, Berkeley, Calif.: University of California Press, 1968.

Garvey, Catherine. *Play*, Cambridge, Mass.: Harvard University Press, 1977.

Kirshenblatt-Gimblett, Barbara (ed.). *Speech Play: Research and Resources for the Study of Linguistic Creativity*, Philadelphia: University of Pennsylvania Press, 1976.

4

Nonverbal Communication

When Jennie was 1:11 her mother reported that Jennie's grandparents had kept her older brothers overnight but had not kept her. She pouted all the way home. When her grandparents brought the boys home the next day, Jennie climbed up on her grandfather's lap and did not move until they were ready to leave. Then she marched out the door to their car. As soon as her grandfather opened the door for the dog to get in, Jennie scrambled up onto the back seat and tried to buckle the seat belt. She communicated her intention to go home with them, and she went!

There are a number of messages that can be acted out—communicated entirely without words—for either an almost-two-year-old or an adult. It has been suggested that man's first language was gestural, and it has remained the case that nonverbal aspects of communication are vital. Key[1] contends that "whatever language, or whatever the purpose in communication, informational or expressive, emotions and attitudes *always* project themselves in an overlay of superimposed patterns." If gestural language is so basic that verbal language evolved from it, and emotions and attitudes are always projected by nonverbal means, it is not surprising to find that children acquire a nonverbal system of communication before the verbal system. In spite of its early appearance and its pervasiveness, we have been persistently ignorant about nonverbal communication even as we have become more sophisticated about outer space, artificial intelligence, and scientific matters in general.

We are just now watching the initial stages of a revolution in the methods used to study human behavior, particularly where language is concerned. The advent of the portable magnetic-tape video recorder has opened new vistas for social science research in recent years. The advantage of simultaneous picture and sound recording which is instantly replayable, over the use of photographic film, is substantial. Impetus in the use of video recording equipment by educational and research organizations was given in the late 1960s by many equipment purchase grants from agencies of the federal government. The experiences of early users of videotape recorders aroused an interest in this type of research data gathering that did not exist when only the photographic process was available.

Results of some of this research are reported in this chapter.

Terminology: In this chapter, *verbal* means spoken words. The pitch, volume, stress, lengthening, hesitation, tempo, and other factors that go into "tone of voice" are considered to be part of the *nonverbal* factor of language, usually referred to as *paralinguistic* features of language, or as Key[2] puts it, "the vocal sounds of nonverbal communication." It may be seen readily that it is the paralinguistic features that determine the meaning of many utterances. Try saying "your brother" with various stress and intonation patterns, etc., and listen to the meaning change while the words remain the same. "*Your* brother!" = "He is *not* your brother!"; "Your *bro*ther?" = "You mean your boy friend!"; "Your brother" (neither word stressed) = "Your brother" (as an answer to "Who was that on the phone?"), etc.

The first aspect of nonverbal communication to be considered in this chapter will be nonlanguage vocal behavior, or the vocal sounds of nonverbal communication. The second aspect will be body movement and orientation, usually referred to as *kinesics*. Third is personal space, or *proxemics*, a term coined by Edward Hall[3] "for the interrelated observations and theories of man's use of space as a specialized elaboration of culture."

Gesticulation (not treated in this chapter), such as is used while speaking to complement the verbal message, has received remarkably little attention from researchers, except for a study by Long and von

Raffler-Engel.[4] They found that children who were the most talkative also did the most gesticulating. Schmidt and Hore[5] hypothesized that children who were more proficient with the verbal-linguistic means of communicating would make less use of nonverbal means in their communication with others, whereas children with less command of verbal language would make greater use of nonverbal channels. Specifically, they looked at body closeness without contact and at glancing behavior. The results of their experiment did not bear out their hypothesis, however. Rather, they found that individuals who used a more complex level of verbal communication also employ at least one of the nonverbal channels—namely, glancing behavior—to a greater extent in storytelling (at least). This was a limited situation, but indications are that children do not use nonverbal means of communication because they lack language. Quite the contrary. The effective communicator uses both means effectively.

Children are effective users of nonverbal communication before they begin to produce language, as well as after. The communication of meaning is not as dependent upon words as we have sometimes thought.

The Vocal Sounds of Nonverbal Communication

Crying is the first nonverbal vocal sound produced by children, and other sounds, such as cooing and babbling, follow. These sounds are not always without meaning. They may express pain as opposed to hunger, happiness, contentment, etc., and can often be translated quite accurately by the child's principal caretaker. As indicated in Chapter 2, when mothers chat with babies as young as six to eight weeks of age, the child's vocalizations may often be interpreted as an attempt by children to interact with their mothers (prelinguistic conversations). Infant vocalizations are precursors of language; some of them eventually lead to language sounds; some result in paralinguistic phenomena (aspects of nonverbal communication).

Children not only use nonverbal features of language, they respond to them long before they understand the words spoken to them. They understand the meaning of a stern voice, sometimes even when the speaker doesn't think it is very stern. At five months, Kara cried when she was asked "Do you have a wet diaper?" Barb insisted she was smiling and using a soft voice, but Kara detected an edge to the question, and responded by crying; up until then she had been happy all day. In contrast to such a direct question, adults often use baby talk and an unusually high pitch as a way of talking affectionately to children. This "how" something is said is more important in determining the response from a child than "what" is said.

Intonation Patterns   Many children (certainly not all) use sentence-like intonation patterns with their babbling,[6] sometimes as early as five months of age. By the time children are producing meaningful utterances, suitable intonation patterns usually accompany them. It seems clear in many cases that children have intonation contours they don't yet have words for. By 1:9, whenever Leslie wanted to say something that went beyond her vocabulary, she communicated with intonation. She did this most often when she was very pleased or excited. She usually started her sentence with the name of the person she was addressing as a means of getting their attention, then completed the sentence with *ga ga*'s, for example, "Mommy! gagaga gaga gagagaga!" At this same age she also had a "counting" intonation which she used for pointing to objects on each page of her counting book. For this she used only vowels, and as she pronounced each of five vowels, she used a rising intonation and then paused before she went on to the next vowel.

We often find children using deviant intonation patterns as a way of expressing meaning. For example, between the ages of about 2:10 and 3:2, Leslie frequently used a lowering intonation pattern to indicate negative meaning in utterances that had no negative morpheme (such as *no* or *not*). In such cases, the utterance not only had a steadily lowering pitch, but she lowered her head as the sentence progressed so that her chin was almost to her chest by the time she finished a relatively long sentence. She also opened her eyes wider than usual, which is a gestural aspect of negation sometimes used by adults, particularly when addressing children, such as in warning or prohibition situations, for example, "I don't think you should do that!" For example:

> Leslie (3:0): /i bɛg hurt mi e o mi/ (Lady bug won't hurt me. They love me.)
> /e wrn i kɛr mi/ (A worm doesn't scare me.)
> To be certain of her meaning, I asked, "Don't worms scare you?" and she answered,
> /no e o mi/ (No, they love me.)

Whereas normally in a declarative sentence only the last morpheme of Leslie's sentences had a falling intonation, when she intended a negative meaning such as the above, everything beyond the subject carried a lowering intonation.

Lord[7] reported that her daughter Jennifer, at 2:0, used a rising intonation to indicate negation, in which the subject was at a normal level, and the remainder of the utterance continued to rise. "I want need help" with a rising intonation meant "I don't need help!"

Such patterns are probably not entirely idiosyncratic but are determined by the patterns associated with negation that each child heard most frequently. Either pattern mentioned above is possible in adult speech.

Children offer clear indications that intonation contours are meaningful to them, both those they hear and those they produce.

Pitch In a study of the use of various paralinguistic features by young children, I found that they were using high pitch in talking to babies or about babies or in addressing pets, much as adults do in using baby talk. For example, when Leslie was 0:6, Fred addressed her in a high-pitched voice:

> Fred (3:10): Hi Lesh! How are you? Oh, you're laugh—
> playing laughing all the time! Why? Why? Why? Can you
> shake hands? How come you laugh all the time? How
> come?

His language also included other baby talk register features such as an exaggerated intonation pattern and some phonetic modification (Les → Lesh; changing an *s* to an *sh* sound was one of Fred's usual ways to mark baby talk).

From about 2:0 to 2:6, John used high pitch in talking to their parakeet, and at 3:1, he addressed their dog in a high pitch:

> John: Archie, what can you do? Can you just bark? Or just
> sing? Can you sing?

In the case of both boys, it is obvious that they were not expecting an answer from either the six-month-old baby or the dog. They were using high-pitched voices as a means of expressing affection. Neither of them would have addressed a peer or an older person in the same way.

Leslie regularly (2:6 to 4:6) used high pitch when she was playing with dolls and pretending the doll was talking. And both Fred and Leslie used high pitch when they were reporting things that had happened to themselves at a much younger age. For example, Leslie was telling about how she could "get out of the fence," meaning climb over the little fence which was in the doorway to her room. I asked, "You could get out of what?" She replied in a high-pitched voice:

Leslie (4:1): Out of a fence. If I was two again.

Leslie's first name for a doll was *gigi,* and she said "gigi" in a high pitch whenever she referred to her "baby."

In addition to using high pitch for talking to babies or about babies, the children I have observed also use it when they are very uncertain or for excitement, but it is not used randomly. When the listener notes that the child has switched from a normal pitch to high pitch, he may assume that it connotes something special to the child.

Whispering   Another paralinguistic feature (though technically not a *vocal* sound of nonverbal communication) is whispering, in which sounds are articulated as usual but they are unvoiced. Whispering is a medium of secrets for adults, and for children as well, though I have found that children vary dramatically in the age at which they learn to whisper. Leslie and John started to use whispering at about the same time they started to talk, whereas Fred was 4:6 when he was first noted using it. By the time John was 2:6, he started whispering to parents if they were visiting someone and he wanted to make a request, such as for a drink of water; he then expected his parents to make the request for him. He also used whispering when he was concentrating, as in self-directed speech, where Fred used a soft voice.

Differences in the ages at which children learn to whisper and their inclination to use it at appropriate times seem to be closely related to personality differences.

Body Movement (Kinesics)

The discussion in this section will be limited to *message-related movements*[8] and will include (1) explicit gestures (called *emblems* by Ekman and Friesen[9]) such as waving goodbye or putting one's finger to the lips as a signal to be quiet; (2) body postures (implicit gestures) which convey messages but which are not as well defined in society as explicit gestures; (3) body rhythms as they relate to those of others; and (4) facial expressions, gaze direction, and eye contact.

Explicit Gestures   Before they are producing any words at all, children usually have a repertoire of at least a dozen or so gestures that can be easily translated by the parents or caretaker, and usually by any careful observer. Such gestures include: standing in front of a person and lifting up both arms = pick me up; waving an arm = good-bye; holding out doll and dress = put the dress on the doll; taking empty glass to refrigerator = give me more milk. Such gestures are so common and so easily understood in context that Haselkorn[10] found in a study of eleven children ranging in age from twelve to eighteen months that requests made by the child to either the mother or the experimenter were interpreted no more easily when the child added language than when requests were made nonverbally. She reported, "We must conclude that language is simply making no difference with respect to how certain an observer is about a child's request. This finding suggests that the adult is interpreting the child's requests on the basis of the child's nonverbal behavior and its context whether or not a verbalization or vocalization is included." At this age, adults did not seem to take the child's object names at face value but considered the nonverbal cue to be primary. Hazelkorn concluded that early language does not replace nonverbal communication but is redundant with such strategies.

At any age, when a listener notes that gestures and intonation contradict language, the listener is inclined to believe the nonverbal communication. Gestures are powerful communicators.

Specific gestures are sometimes used and well understood within a family or small speech community without being widely understood at all. For example, at 2:6 to 2:10, when Jennie was asked to call her brothers to dinner, she ran to their door, stood on one foot with the other foot lifted and extended backward as she held onto the door casing, and shouted "ah!" The loud voice plus the *calling stance*, which was used at no other time, signaled "calling" to her older brothers. They correctly interpreted it as "Mother says come."

Greetings, which are found in all cultures of the world, often incorporate gestures. In our culture, adults shake hands as part of a greeting, and boys as young as two or three years of age are sometimes taught to shake hands. Brandon devised his own nonverbal greeting for me and for his parents (see Chapter 2), but children are usually taught some greeting behavior, such as hugging or kissing family members and saying "Hi" to others.

Body Postures   The way persons stand, sit, or orient their bodies toward other persons can indicate how well they like the other person, whether they feel superior or inferior, and when they are fighting, may indicate by body posture when they are ready to quit, etc. Some messages are usually thought of as implicit rather than explicit, such as waving good-bye. A person may be aware that another person seems to like him but be unaware that the forward-leaning torso and a body orientation facing rather than standing at angles was what gave the impression. Such body postures are not assumed consciously, nor are they ordinarily interpreted consciously. As Sapir[11] noted, "We respond to gestures with an extreme alertness and, one might say, in accordance with an elaborate code that is written nowhere, known by none, yet understood by all."

In a series of interesting studies by Ginsburg,[12] it was found that body postures which most of us are only dimly aware of were signals for the fighting between schoolboys to stop. One hundred and eight sixth-grade boys were observed unobtrusively over a 12-week period during their hourly recess periods, and a videotape recorder was activated whenever the initial occurrence of a fight was noted. In 60 hours of observation, 281 skirmishes were taped; of these, 46 were concluded because a third child—an onlooker—intervened. Typically the child giving aid jumped on the back of the aggressor, allowing the child under attack an opportunity to escape. Why did the onlooker intervene? Ginsburg initially assumed that the intervention took place because the third child was a good friend of the child being attacked, but a close examination of the videotape records suggested a much more intriguing explanation. It appeared that aid was given when the aggressor continued to attack after the child under attack had given an "appeasement display"—a body posture that served to communicate a "request for cease fire." Ginsburg reports that "nonverbal requests for the cessation of fighting were forms of diminution of structure, such as "head-bowing, shoulder slumping (where the child lowers his shoulders and bends forward), lying motionless on the ground, and, curiously enough, shoe-tying." Bowing, kneeling, prostration, etc., are gestures of ritualized appeasement in many human cultures and are indications of the subordination of certain individuals to those of higher rank, or more powerful members of the social order. Thus, Ginsburg points out, "The communicative function of such nonverbal displays during fights between children appears to be 'All right already, enough is enough, you win!' " Most of the schoolground fights stopped when such a gesture of diminution was used by the child under attack, but when the aggressor ignored the signal to stop, another child interceded.

Ginsburg[13] describes the analysis of the behavior:

> Analysis of this situation focused upon the ongoing interaction between the aggressor and the child being attacked just prior to the onset of aid giving. The pattern of behavior which precipitated altruism was measured by

occluding from view a portion of the playback monitor so that a naive observer could see the intervening child, but could not see the two children engaged in the fight. The observer was asked to stop the tape at the point immediately preceding the onset of aid-giving. This stop-action frame was simultaneously provided to three naive observers who were asked to determine the activity of the aggressor (continued attack or no attack) and the activity of the other child (striking back, kneeling, etc.).

It was predicted that altruism was most likely to occur if the aggressor continued his assault in spite of a nonverbal communication of submission (via diminished body posture) by the child under attack. Thirty-eight of the 46 episodes resulted in complete agreement by the three raters in terms of the types of activities exhibited by the two children just prior to the onset of intervention. Thirty-one of the 38 episodes involved continued aggression by the antagonist while the child under attack exhibited one of the previously mentioned appeasement displays (kneel, head bow, shoulder slump, head bow combined with shoulder slump, prostration, or shoe-tying). It thus appears that an act of altruism in the context of children's playground activity has an extremely high probability of occurrence if the aggressor fails to heed a nonverbal signal communicating submission.

In a subsequent study using the same data, Ginsburg asked a different group of children (fourth and fifth graders, both boys and girls) to view (individually) segments of the videotaped fights, some of which ended of their own accord and some of which were ended when a third child intervened. The children were not shown the portion of the videotape on which the fight actually ended, and they were asked to state if they thought a third child would give assistance to the child under attack. To determine what cues were involved in correctly predicting an act of altruism, the children were asked to state the reason for their judgments. The results indicated that the children were usually able to predict correctly when another child would intercede, but they were unable to verbalize in any precise manner the reason for their judgments.

Ginsburg asked if it might be that the child under attack was not transmitting effective cues of submission, thus resulting in the persistence of the aggressor in his attack. However, the general agreement of the children that the nonverbal signs were clear suggests that the aggressor ignored the message, rather than simply not receiving it.

Cross-Cultural Study of Postures: French-English bilingual children studied by von Raffler-Engel[14] were found to have separate kinesic systems for their two cultures. The systems, interestingly, did not necessarily change when they changed language but changed when the speaker was addressing a person of the other culture. Von Raffler-Engel states:[15]

> In code switching, the Anglophone children maintain their own customary kinetic system, but sometimes intersperse it with exaggerated Francophone kinesics. Over-correctness is particularly evident when the children are not completely fluent in the French language.
>
> The Francophone children do not correlate kinesics with language code switching. They correlate kinesics with ethnic group switching. When speaking either French or English with an Anglophone, they will employ a reduced version of their own customary kinesics. When speaking English to Francophones (this instance is more frequent than outsiders would presume), they maintain their previous relaxed attitude and do not alter their native kinesics.
>
> The sociolinguistic implications of the different cues of relationship between language and culture among Canada's two ethnic groups are profound and merit further investigation:
>
> 1. a. French children signal their readiness for a friendly chat by leaning forward toward each other while English children convey the same message by leaning back on the chair and extending their feet in a relaxed manner.
>   b. Francophone children underscore what they say with paralinguistic gestures on the word level. They do this particularly with qualifiers, adjectives and adverbs. Anglophone children act out whole situations. They employ what could be termed discourse paralinguistics. The difference in paralinguistic behavior between the two ethnic groups is striking: the gestures of Francophones are strictly language-related while Anglophone children act out a theme which they also describe

verbally at the same time. Their gestures are discourse-related rather than word-related.

2. a. When Francophone children speak either French or English to Anglophones they tend to modify their customary kinetics. They lean forward, but only slightly, and they make far less frequent use of paralinguistic gestures. When they do employ these gestures, they spread their hands less expansively.

   b. When Anglophone children speak English to Francophones, their kinetics do not differ from when they speak to Anglophones. When speaking French either to another Anglophone—as would be the case in practicing for their school work—or to a Francophone, these children make an effort at copying some kinetic features of the Francophone population. The features copied appear at random but are consistently exaggerated.

Von Raffler-Engel concludes from her extensive research of the kinesic behavior of bilingual and bidialectal children that appropriate body postures (ranging from formal to informal) for conversation with persons of various ages and in various situations are learned at a very early age and that variation in behavior is not dependent entirely upon the language or dialect spoken, as has sometimes been thought, but on the total complex of the social relationship involved.

Body Rhythms   Among the most fascinating of all studies of nonverbal communication are those that have revealed the extent to which we move in concert with others without an awareness of it. Von Raffler-Engel,[16] for example, videotaped seven children aged three to thirteen and their two sets of parents, and found that they changed posture, usually shifting weight from one foot to the other, when the conversation reached a new topic. Subtopics generally elicited only a slight head movement, but examination of the videotapes revealed that such changes in topic were easily identified by watching body movements. No body movements were detected at the end of sentences, however. There is other evidence that children aged three and even younger know when they are changing the topic, but it is interesting to find that they indicate it nonverbally in the same way that adults do, with both the listener and the speaker moving in concert. In a study with adults, it has been found that the parallel between the speaker's speech and listener's body movements (changes in posture at a topic change, etc.) is greater when the listener is attracted to the speaker than when this attraction is absent.

The Face and Eyes   In terms of nonverbal communication, the most communicative area of the body is the face and particularly the eyes. The face is usually considered to be the principal communicator of moods or emotions—a much more reliable indicator than language. Six "basic" emotions have been identified: happiness, anger, fear, sadness, surprise, and disgust. Of these, at least happiness is recognized from one culture to the next by means of facial expression.

Research in the communicative effectiveness of facial expression ranges from difficult to impossible with adult subjects, and I know of no substantive research in the area with children. We need no research, however, to help us translate messages of mood changes, etc., in the children we deal with on a regular basis. Because young children have not yet learned to mask their feelings, we have no doubt about their expressions of happiness, sadness, anger, etc., and find such readings more accurate than those of adult facial expressions.

Eye Contact and Gaze Direction: There is a special kind of communication that takes place when the eyes of two persons meet. Very young infants participate in such behavior, and eye contact expressing affection is an important element in the infant's emotional development. From infancy on, a child is given very subtle instruction regarding eye contact and gaze direction, and before children are of school age they have learned when to avert their gaze and when to look a person "in the eye." Unfortunately for cross-cultural communication, what children growing up in different cultures learn may be quite different. American children are taught to look at an adult who is instructing or chastising them, while a Puerto Rican child looks at an adult who is instructing him but looks respectfully down when being chastised—to look the chastising person "in the eye" would seem challenging, arrogant, and disrespectful. The black child learns to look at a person to whom he is talking but to look away when someone is talking to him; a white child learns the opposite—to look away (most of the time) when he is talking to someone but to watch attentively while listening. In Japan, Taylor[17] says "parents train each child not to burden other people with his problems by letting his feelings show in his face. He is taught to avert his eyes to show respect. The American thinks he sees familiar body language but completely misses the respect and agreeableness the Japanese is trying to convey."

Possibilities for misunderstanding abound because we are not even aware of our own customs, much less those of other cultures. Hall[18] presses for wider understanding of the "out-of-awareness" aspects of communication. He says, "We must never assume that we are fully aware of what we communicate to someone else. There exist in the world today tremendous distortions in meaning as men try to communicate with one another. The job of achieving understanding and insight into mental processes of others is much more difficult and the situation more serious than most of us care to admit."

More universal behaviors regarding eye contact and gaze direction include the insistence of deaf persons on eye contact in interactions; they rely heavily on eye contact and other kinesic movement to supplement their conversations. Robert Shields, the talented mime, reports "When I stare at somebody, without blinking, it completely disarms them. I've met nobody who can handle it." Unrelieved staring makes us uncomfortable. And just as eye contact carries with it a special kind of communication, the complete avoidance of eye contact signals something special—social distance, a disinclination to be friendly, or outright unfriendliness.

Key[19] mentions that the eye can be used as a "regulator" in conversations in an informal way, and it can be used in a more precise way, for example, as a signal between the chairman of a meeting and a member who is asking for the floor. In a similar vein, in a classroom, students who know the answer to a question the teacher has just asked will generally try to "catch the teacher's eye," while the students who do not know the answer will avoid eye contact. And anyone who has ever lived through a year in the formal kind of classroom where children are not supposed to talk will remember the many meaningful glances exchanged across the room as "asides" while the teacher was talking, or by way of discussing more personal matters.

Personal Space (Proxemics)

Most of us have always been aware of our own personal space, but until Edward T. Hall coined the word *proxemics*, it was less common to talk about it. One of the interesting observations Hall made is that there are "contact" and "noncontact" cultures. We are not aware of the importance of these norms until they are violated, and this happens typically in cross-cultural interaction. We don't place the same meaning on the same proxemic behavior. Arabs, for example, belong to a "contact" culture.[20] They stand close together, and when we get together with them, they may stand uncomfortably close to us. One young college man was relieved to hear this, as he had thought his Arab roommate was homosexual. Arabs gaze into our eyes for longer than we are comfortable with, standing directly in front of us, touching our bodies with their hands or bodies, breathing on our faces. We consider it to be aggressive and generally unpleasant. We may not even be consciously aware of what the problem is. We are not accustomed to thinking, "Now, I want you to stand 18 inches away from me. If you stand only 12 inches away, I will think you are being aggressive." We cannot anlayze the behavior; we just react to it.

Children are aware of their space, too. It is not unusual for children to object to someone else sitting or playing in a space adjacent to where they are sitting or playing. They don't offer any reasons for their objections, and their mothers will often force them to allow a playmate to play as close as he wants to. There is often no obvious reason for the child to have marked off a circle, as it were. He is not actively using the space, any more than we actively use the space for 18 inches around us. We just consider it ours.

Cross-Cultural Differences   To what extent are proxemic relationships a potential source of misunderstanding in face-to-face cross-cultural exchanges, and at what age do such differences in such proxemic relationships appear? Aiello and Jones[21] decided to examine the proxemic behavior of three groups of six- to eight-year-old children in New York City: Puerto Rican, black, and white. A total of 420 children (210 pairs) were chosen, equal numbers of male and female so that there were 35 samples taken from each sex-culture group. The black and Puerto Rican children were from a lower-socioeconomic-class elementary school in the South Bronx area of New York City and the white children were from a middle-class elementary school just outside New York City in Nassau County.

Observers were trained to judge not only the distance in inches that the children were standing from each other when talking to each other but also the angle at which they stood. An 8-point axis, much like that of a compass, was used to estimate the children's position relative to that of the conversational partner. The most "direct" position possible is facing the other child; shoulders at right angles is a less direct position, and a position in which both children faced the same direction while talking is the least direct (children were not observed facing away from each other while talking to each other).

What they found was that white children stand farther apart while talking to each other than black or Puerto Rican children do, but they face each other more directly. It may be seen, then, that there is a certain degree of equivalence between standing farther apart and facing a partner head on and standing closer together but facing the same direction or standing at only a slight angle to each other. Aiello and Jones suggest that "It could be that although some homogeneous *degree* of nonverbal expression prevails across cultures, the particular *mode* of expression varies from culture to culture."

They also found that white boys stood farther apart than white girls, but that there were no sex differences in the black and Puerto Rican subcultures.

Inasmuch as there were no significant differences between the black and Puerto Rican children, the authors suggest that the variation in the groups may be found in social class rather than culture per se. That is, lower class are different from middle class, rather than black and Puerto Ricans being different than whites. Either way, it is interesting that consistent differences were found during childhood.

Summary

It is often assumed that words convey our messages. Why else would we use them? But they convey a message only to the extent that the nonverbal message agrees with the verbal message. Gestural language, it has been suggested, is what verbal language evolved from, and is vital to the communication process.

Figure 3 indicates an estimate of the order in which some nonverbal aspects of communication are acquired, and an estimate of the age at which some children have been observed using them. No norms have been established for the ages at which such capabilities may be acquired, nor are there likely to be, for both cultural and individual differences will always exist.

Paralinguistic features of language, or the vocal sounds of nonverbal communication, include pitch, volume, stress, intonation contours, etc., and determine much of the meaning of verbal language. It is generally thought that it is the paralinguistic aspects of language that children respond to at earliest ages. Long before children know what words mean, they understand the feeling conveyed by the paralinguistic features of the language directed to them. This is also what they produce first. Once children have acquired language, they may use some aspects of paralanguage idiosyncratically to convey meaning, such as using a lowering intonation pattern to indicate negation before they are able to include *no* or *not* in the utterance.

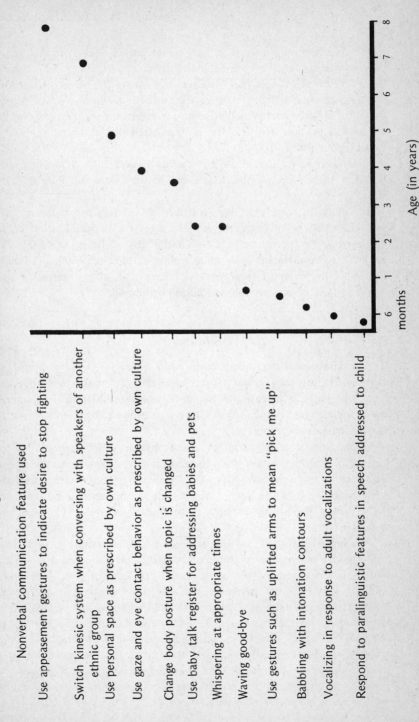

Figure 3 Estimate of Age at Which Children Acquire Capability of Using Certain Aspects of Nonverbal Communication

A review of available data indicates that young children use body movement (kinesics) in many of the same ways adults do. They use many explicit gestures, such as waving good-bye or standing in front of a person and lifting up their arms to indicate that they wish to be picked up. They also use implicit gestures, which are not well defined in our society but which are nevertheless well understood by everyone. A study of fighting on the schoolground by boys revealed that when the boy under attack was ready to give up, he gave a nonverbal request for the cessation of fighting in the form of diminution of structure: head-bowing, shoulder slumping, lying motionless on the ground, and even shoe-tying. When this signal was not heeded by the aggressor, it was found that another child often interceded to stop the fight—the observing child recognized the "appeasement display" and became indignant that the aggressor paid no attention to it. The boys who stopped the fighting, however, were unable to verbalize in any precise manner the reason for their intercession. Such nonverbal messages are out-of-the-awareness of those who use them.

French-English bilingual children were found to have separate kinesic systems for each language, but were found not to switch them when they switched languages but to switch according to the ethnicity of their conversational partner.

It has been found that children, as well as adults, change body posture when the topic of the conversation they are engaged in changes; no change is made for the end of sentences; a slight head movement accompanies a new subtopic; and a shift in weight from one foot to the other often accompanies a topic change.

From a communicative point of view, the most important area of the body is the face, and particularly the eyes. Infants learn to read facial expressions, and because they do not learn at early ages to mask their feelings, we can usually judge a child's facial expressions of happiness, sadness, anger, etc., rather accurately.

From infancy on, children are given very subtle instruction regarding eye contact and gaze direction. This varies considerably from culture to culture.

Such research as has been conducted in the area of personal space (proxemics) indicates that children develop this sense at an early age. Cross-cultural differences between groups of six- to eight-year-old black, white, and Puerto Rican children were observed in the distance the children stood from each other when talking, as well as the angle at which they stood.

It is apparent that the elaborate code of gestures referred to by Sapir that is "written nowhere, known by none, yet understood by all" is learned early in life.

NOTES

1. Key, Mary Ritchie. *Paralanguage and Kinesics*, Metuchen, N.J.: Scarecrow Press, 1975, p. 9.

2. *Ibid.*, p. 41.

3. Hall, Edward T., "A System of Notation of Proxemic Behavior," *American Anthropologist*, 1963, 65:109-116.

4. Long, Lucy, and Walburga von Raffler-Engel. "A Correlation of Verbal and Non-verbal Behavior in Black and White Children in a Day Care Center in Nashville, Tenn.," unpublished manuscript, 1968.

5. Schmidt, Wilfred H. O., and Terence Hore. "Some Nonverbal Aspects of Communication between Mother and Preschool Child," *Child Development*, 1970, 41:889-896.

6. Some babies do not babble. Jennie was such a child, but as mentioned in Chapter 3, she babbled at a much later age. Kara, who is almost eleven months old at this writing, was another nonbabbler up to this age, but is now babbling a little.

7. Lord, Carol. "Variations in the Pattern of Acquisition of Negation," paper presented at the Sixth Annual Child Language Research Forum, April 6, 1974, Stanford University, Stanford, Calif.

8. This terminology is borrowed from Walburga von Raffler-Engel, "Development Kinescis: Cultural Differences in the Acquisition of Nonverbal Behavior," in *Child Language—1975*, edited by Walburga von Raffler-Engel, International Linguistic Association, 1976. (Special issue of *Word*, 1971, 27:195-204.)

9. Ekman, Paul, and Wallace V. Friesen. "The Repertoire of Nonverbal Behavior: Categories, Origins, Usage, and Coding," *Semiotica*, 1969, 1:49-98.

10. Haselkorn, Sharon L. "The Relationship of Verbal to Preverbal Strategies," paper presented at the Second Annual Boston University Conference on Language Development, Boston, September 1977.

11. Sapir, Edward. "The Unconscious Patterning of Behavior in Society," in *The Unconscious: A Sympoisum*, edited by E. S. Drummer, New York: Knopf, 1927.

12. Ginsburg, Harvey J. "Altruism in Children: The Significance of Nonverbal Behavior," *Journal of Communication*, 1977, 27 (4):82-86.

13. *Ibid.*, p. 84.

14. von Raffler-Engel, Walburga. "Some Rules of Socio-Kinesics," *Proceedings of the Fourth International Congress of Applied Linguistics*, Hochschul Verlag, Stuttgart, 1976.

15. *Ibid.*, pp. 115-116.

16. von Raffler-Engel, Walburga: "Kinesics and Topic," *Language Sciences*, 1975, 37:39.

17. Taylor, Harvey M. "Japanese Kinesics," *Journal of the Associated Teachers of Japanese*, 1974, 9 (1):65-76.

18. Hall, Edward T. *The Silent Language*, Garden City, N.Y.: Anchor Press, 1973.

19. *Paralanguage and Kinesics*.

20. Watson, O. M., and T. D. Graves ("Quantitative Research in Proxemic Behavior," *American Anthropologist*, 1966, 68:971-985) found differences in spatial orientation (distance, shoulder orientation, and eye contact) between Arab and American cultures and among geographical regions within these cultures.

21. Aiello, John R., and Stanley E. Jones. "Field Study of the Proxemic Behavior of Young Children in Three Subcultural Groups," *Journal of Personality and Social Psychology*, 1971, 19:351-356.

SUGGESTED READINGS

Hall, Edward T. *The Silent Language.* Garden City, N.Y.: Anchor Press, 1973.

von Raffler-Engel, Walburga, and Bates Hoffer. *Aspects of Nonverbal Communication: A Handbook*, San Antonio, Tex.: Linguistic Department, Trinity University, 1977.

Schlesinger, Hilde S., and Kathryn P. Meadow. *Sound and Sign: Childhood Deafness and Mental Health*, Berkeley, University of California Press, 1972.

Wilkinson, Andrew. *Language and Education*, London: Oxford University Press, 1975.

EPILOGUE

I have discussed in this book some of the aspects of language used by young children. What I believe are essentially all the functions of child language were discussed in Chapter 1, some of these were discussed more fully in Chapters 2 and 3, and in Chapter 4 I discussed how children accomplish some of these same purposes in a nonverbal mode.

What I hope I have done is to show that the language system used by children to accomplish their goals is remarkably complex from infancy on. And when I say "language system," I am including the semantic system that develops long before there are any words at all. Including this system is the only way we can account for the prelanguage communicative competence of young children. For example, I am impressed that at six months of age, Margaret Ann babbles only when no one in the room is talking, but she plays silently when others are talking. I am impressed that Brandon took it upon himself to tell Kara that a certain ball was a doggie ball before he had the words, other than "oof," with which to do the job. And that Leslie would set out to tell her mother a joke ("Mommy, gagagagagaga?" laughing as she chattered) before she had words with which to do it. The language produced is obviously not too impressive; what is impressive is the evidence of the rapidly developing semantic systems that "words," when acquired, will fit into. I have tried to make the point throughout the book that language consists of much more than words. Children as young as Brandon and Kara have rules that specify that one approaches a person one wishes to converse with, one gets their attention, one uses sentence melodies with babbling when words are not available, one uses appropriate pitch and volume, as starters. Rule-systems, even at this age, are obviously extremely complicated.

We have also seen time and again throughout the book that experience is the key to early linguistic sophistication. While all children are born into the same world, different children see different portions of it; and while every child has one or more caretakers, the characteristics of such individuals may vary dramatically. A child born into a large, affectionate, extended family will have a different view of the world than a child born to an unmarried girl who does not want a child and has no means of supporting one. Likewise children born in a hogan on the desert, in a mountain cabin, on a farm, in a castle on the Rhine, or in a city tenement may have different views of the world. The kind of speech community the child is born into will be different in each of the above cases, and the child's language patterns will differ accordingly. There are innumerable factors that will affect the experiences a child has: the kind of language directed to the child; whether or not the child has attentive listeners; the age of persons with whom the child may interact; the amount of time the child spends alone or with other persons; the child's rank in the family; the availability of stimulating objects and events in the child's environment, etc.

We have also seen that no matter what kind of home children are born into, and no matter where, they are born with certain characteristics that are uniquely their own. It is not at all a matter of whether nature or nurture is more important; they are equally important. We see that Fred and Leslie's language development was very different even though they grew up in the same home; nothing could have changed this dramatically, though we can imagine how a different home situation might have changed the language development of each of them somewhat.

It is my hope that parents and others who work with children will be stimulated by this book to appreciate more fully the amazing complexity of the language of children—one of the exciting wonders of the world.

GLOSSARY

Alliteration   The repetition, usually of an initial consonant, in two or more neighboring words or syllables, as in sing a song of sixpence.

Anglophone   A speaker of English.

Babbling   Speech-type sounds that are made principally during the prespeech period of infancy (from perhaps six months to one year). Babbling may also continue after language has begun. It is often interpreted as attempts at language.

Baby talk   Speech directed to babies (or pets, etc.) by adults or older children, which is patterned according to what the adult thinks is a baby's way of speaking, or a way of speaking which adults think is appropriate for addressing young children, but which is not regarded as normal, adult use of language. This may include phonological modifications, such as *oo* for *you*, morphological modifications, such as *shoesies* for *shoes*, or lexical changes, such as *choo-choo* for *train*.

Contingent query   A request, during the course of conversation, for clarification of something that was not understood by the listener or not fully specified by the speaker. This request, the response to it, and the acknowledgment of the response represent a digression from the conversation, are subordinate to it, and contingent upon it.

Egocentric speech   A term used by Piaget to refer to speech that a child directs to himself. If the child assumes others are listening, he "does not attempt to place himself at the point of view of his hearer." It is the opposite of *socialized* speech, which is directed to other persons (see p. 76). In this book, egocentric speech is usually referred to as *noncommunicative* while socialized speech is referred to as *communicative*.

Francophone   A speaker of French.

Heuristic   Serving to guide, reveal, or discover.

Intonation patterns (or contours)   Patterns in the modulation of the voice, including pitch and tone quality; the musical flow of speech.

Kinesics   The study of nonvocal body movements and orientation, including automatic reflexes, posture, facial expressions, gestures, etc., which play a part in communication.

Lexical   Relating to the total stock of morphemes or words in a given language. (A *lexical item* is a word.)

Longitudinal study   One that spans a period of time—anywhere from several weeks to several years.

Marked/unmarked   The original linguistic theory of marked versus unmarked features in phonology (the sound system of the language) has been generalized to other aspects of language. In phonology oral vowels may be considered as *unmarked* while nasal vowels are *marked*. All languages have oral vowels, and they may, in addition, have nasal vowels, or they may not. No language has nasal vowels without also having oral vowels. The oral vowels, or the unmarked member of the pair oral/nasal, are the more basic. In grammar, of the pair singular/plural, the singular is the unmarked member of the pair; the plural is generally marked in English with a suffixed -*s*.

Metalanguage   Language that is used to talk about language.

Monologue   A long speech uttered by one person while one or more persons listen.

Monoreme   A one-word utterance.

Morpheme   The smallest individually meaningful element in a language, for example, *clearest* consists of two morphemes: *clear* and *est* (meaning *most*); *cats* consists of two morphemes: *cat* and *s* (meaning *more than one*, or *plural*).

Onomatopoeic   Imitative in origin; echoic.

Paralinguistic   Features of language such as pitch of voice, volume, intonation patterns, and duration. Most paralinguistic features are not tied directly to a sound, but to some larger unit, such as a syllable, word, or phrase.

Phonology   The study of speech sounds with regard to the functions which they fulfill in language.

Proxemics   The study of personal space as a specialized elaboration of culture.

Psycholinguist   An expert in the psychological aspects of language.

Register   Variation in language which depends on the situation or use of the language as opposed to dialect variation, which depends on the social and/or geographical background of the user of the language.

Semantic   Related to meaning in language; the part of language study that describes the meaning of words and sentences.

Soliloquy   A speech uttered in solitude.

Sociolinguistic   Pertaining to the relationship between language and society—to the characteristics of language varieties, their functions, and their speakers, as these three interact with each other, change, and change one another within a speech community.

Stress patterns   Stress consists of special emphasis on a sound or group of sounds, usually by means of extra loudness and lengthening, and sometimes by pitch. Stress patterns evolve as this stress is varied, for example, *Something is very wrong* versus Something is *very* wrong, by first stressing *is* and then stressing *very*.

Syntax   Sentence structure; the part of grammar which describes the relations of words, suffixes, and prefixes to one another as parts of the structure of sentences.

Tag question   A short question which is added to a sentence, and usually functions as a request for verification: *We're going, aren't we?*

or *He didn't do it, did he?* It is syntactically complex, and is sometimes replaced by a simple *huh?* or *right?*

Velar   A consonant formed with the back of the tongue touching or near the velum, or soft palate, such as *g* or *k*.

INDEX